# PRAISE FOR *SOFTWARE CONFIGURATION MANAGEMENT PATTERNS*

I think the authors have just created the new "SCM Bible" that will be the new standard and reference manual for SCM-ers and software development professionals for years and years to come!!

—*Jeffrey W. Faist, Jeff Faist Consulting Inc.*

I'm very glad that people are still writing about SCM. For a while, it seemed that the momentum had shifted away from competence in SCM, and the book writing was following. The organization of this book is quite good, and the content is quite complete. Everything I'd expect from a quality Addison-Wesley piece of work.

—*Craig Gardner*

I think this is a timely book—right now source control is most definitely a black art, and most teams do it badly, if at all. There are very few books on the subject.

—*Dave Thomas, coauthor of* The Pragmatic Programmer: From Journeyman to Master

There's a lot of expertise captured here, and I get a sense of really sitting down with someone who understands these issues.

—*Linda Rising, author of* The Pattern Almanac 2000

I think this is an excellent book. If you're at all serious about software development, you need SCM; this book could make that case and not only convince readers that they need it, but provide enough information that they could immediately apply the patterns on their projects.

—*James Noble, coauthor of* Small Memory Software: Patterns for Systems with Limited Memory

This book is a good overview of a very important area of current software development projects. I say this as someone who has endured (along with my fellow team members) various struggles with SCM systems in the last several companies where I have worked. There is very little readily available literature in this field, and I believe this book will prove to be very important to anyone working in a medium- to large-sized development team.

—*Bernard Farrell, WaveSmith Networks*

# The Software Patterns Series

Series Editor: John M. Vlissides

**The Software Patterns Series** (SPS) comprises pattern literature of lasting significance to software developers. Software patterns document general solutions to recurring problems in all software-related spheres, from the technology itself, to the organizations that develop and distribute it, to the people who use it. Books in the series distill experience from one or more of these areas into a form that software professionals can apply immediately.

*Relevance* and *impact* are the tenets of the SPS. Relevance means each book presents patterns that solve real problems. Patterns worthy of the name are intrinsically relevant; they are borne of practitioners' experiences, not theory or speculation. Patterns have impact when they change how people work for the better. A book becomes a part of the series not just because it embraces these tenets, but because it has demonstrated it fulfills them for its audience.

**Titles in the series:**

*Data Access Patterns: Database Interactions in Object-Oriented Applications*; Clifton Nock

*Design Patterns Explained, Second Edition: A New Perspective on Object-Oriented Design*; Alan Shalloway and James Trott

*Design Patterns in C#*; Steven John Metsker

*Design Patterns in Java™*; Steven John Metsker and William C. Wake

*Design Patterns Java™ Workbook*; Steven John Metsker

*.NET Patterns: Architecture, Design, and Process*; Christian Thilmany

*Pattern Hatching: Design Patterns Applied*; John M. Vlissides

*Pattern Languages of Program Design*; James O. Coplien and Douglas C. Schmidt

*Pattern Languages of Program Design 2*; John M. Vlissides, James O. Coplien, and Norman L. Kerth

*Pattern Languages of Program Design 3*; Robert C. Martin, Dirk Riehle, and Frank Buschmann

*Pattern Languages of Program Design 5*; Dragos Manolescu, Markus Voelter, and James Noble

*Patterns for Parallel Programming*; Timothy G. Mattson, Beverly A. Sanders, and Berna L. Massingill

*Software Configuration Management Patterns: Effective Teamwork, Practical Integration*; Stephen P. Berczuk and Brad Appleton

*The Design Patterns Smalltalk Companion*; Sherman Alpert, Kyle Brown, and Bobby Woolf

*Use Cases: Patterns and Blueprints*; Gunnar Övergaard and Karin Palmkvist

For more information, check out the series web site at www.awprofessional.com/series/swpatterns

# Software Configuration Management Patterns

### Effective Teamwork, Practical Integration

**STEPHEN P. BERCZUK**
**with BRAD APPLETON**

✦Addison-Wesley

*Boston • San Fransisco • New York • Toronto • Montreal*
*London • Munich • Paris • Madrid*
*Capetown • Sydney • Tokyo • Singapore • Mexico City*

Many of the designations used by manufacturers and sellers to distinguish their products are claimed as trademarks. Where those designations appear in this book, and Addison-Wesley was aware of a trademark claim, the designations have been printed with initial capital letters or in all capitals.

The authors and publisher have taken care in the preparation of this book, but make no expressed or implied warranty of any kind and assume no responsibility for errors or omissions. No liability is assumed for incidental or consequential damages in connection with or arising out of the use of the information or programs contained herein.

The publisher offers discounts on this book when ordered in quantity for bulk purchases and special sales. For more information, please contact:

> U.S. Corporate and Government Sales
> (800) 382-3419
> corpsales@pearsontechgroup.com

For sales outside of the U.S., please contact:

> International Sales
> (317) 581-3793
> international@pearsontechgroup.com

Visit Addison-Wesley on the Web: www.awprofessional.com

Library of Congress Cataloging-in-Publication Data

Berczuk, Stephen P.
    Software configuration management patterns : effective teamwork, practical integration
/ Stephen P. Berczuk with Brad Appleton.
       p.  cm.
    Includes bibliographical references and index.
    ISBN 0-201-74117-2 (alk. paper)
    1. Software configuration management.   I. Appleton, Brad.   II. Title.
QA76.76.C69 B465 2002
005.1—dc212002026218

For information on obtaining permission for use of material from this work, please submit a written request to:

> Pearson Education, Inc.
> Rights and Contracts Department
> 75 Arlington Street, Suite 300
> Boston, MA 02116
> Fax: (617) 848-7047

Text printed on recycled and acid-free paper.

ISBN 0201741172
   8 9 10 11 12 OPM 08 07 06
Eighth Printing October 2006

# Contents

# List of Figures

# Foreword

Those of you familiar with my work may be asking yourselves why an expert on J2EE software architecture would be writing a preface for a book on software configuration management (SCM). After all, the two disciplines couldn't be farther apart, could they? J2EE architecture seems lofty and exalted, while SCM might appear to be something that is down in the muck of the trenches of software development. In fact, nothing could be further from the truth. Over the years, I've often found that customers that I work with who have problems with J2EE application architecture usually have serious problems with SCM as well.

The reasons for this curious coincidence are twofold. First, many people have a hard time dealing with change in general—be it moving from a set of architectural practices that no longer apply in a new environment like J2EE, or moving from a software development process that worked in one environment but may not work in all environments as well. Thus they feel that if their SCM processes worked in their last project, they must work in their current project—regardless of the fact that the technologies, timescales, and methods employed in designing and building the two projects may be radically different.

Second, people often want a small set of simple rules to govern all their activities. However, taking a too simple approach usually leads to problems at the edge where abstractions meet reality. Whether the issue is understanding why a particular J2EE construct, such as an Entity EJB, may work in one circumstance but not another, or understanding why it is important for developers to have their own private workspaces in which to do development and integration when, after all, you have to integrate the code from your developers at the end of the day anyway, the problems are the same. In both cases, a simple rule (use Entity beans, use a build script) is perfectly good advice, but it must be tempered in the forge of experience because in its raw form it is too brittle to use.

What mathematicians and scientists have begun to discover in the last two decades of research into chaos and complexity theory is that, although systems built with rules that are too few and too simple are usually stagnant and predictable, adding just a few more rules can often lead to systems of startling complexity and beauty. These are systems that can be seriously perturbed by outside forces and yet can reconstitute themselves so that the overall scheme remains whole. The book you hold in your hand provides a set of rules for SCM that have that kind of flexibility.

Steve and Brad have developed their advice on dealing with SCM as a system of patterns. As they tellingly reveal early on, the strength of a system of patterns lies not in the individual patterns themselves but in the web of relationships between the patterns. The authors have developed an interlocking mesh of patterns that individually cover the most common practices in SCM. However, they more importantly show how the forces that lead to each solution are not completely resolved in each pattern—that you need to carefully consider how each SCM practice is tied to others, to keep from locking yourself into a prison of your own making.

For example, you may want to look ahead to the wonderful advice given in their first pattern, *Mainline (4)*. This seemingly prosaic advice (that developers should work on a single, stable code base) is something that I have found many groups, including those in large, successful corporations that have spent millions of dollars on implementing processes, have somehow failed to grasp. This is common sense, well applied, and that is what makes it uncommon.

Likewise, the advice given in *Private Workspace (6)* and *Private System Build (8)* is nothing less than two of the key ideas that have made modern Java IDEs such as VisualAge for Java and IBM WebSphere Studio so useful and popular. When I am asked (as I am nearly daily) why developers should choose one of these IDEs over development at the command line with traditional code editors and compilers, the fact that these tools not only allow but actively encourage this style of development is a key factor in how I phrase my recommendations.

So, I trust that you find this book as helpful and enlightening as I do. I've been introducing people to a number of the patterns from this book since their first publication in the Pattern Languages of Programs (PLoP) Conference proceedings several years ago, and I've found them to be invaluable in setting the stage for frank and constructive discussions about how to perform SCM the right way. These patterns have been my sword for cutting through the Gordian knot of complex SCM issues in tricky customer engagements—I hope that you will soon begin to wield this weapon as well.

—Kyle Brown
   Author of *Enterprise Java Programming with IBM WebSphere*

# Preface

Software configuration management is not what I do. I am not a software configuration management person. I am not an organizational anthropology person. However, I discovered early on that understanding organizations, software architecture, and configuration management was essential to doing my job as a software developer. I also find this systems perspective on software engineering interesting. I build software systems, and configuration management is a very important and often neglected part of building software systems. In this book, I hope that I can show you how to avoid some of the problems I have encountered so that you can build systems more effectively with your team.

I should probably explain what I mean in distinguishing between software configuration management (SCM) people and people who build software systems. The stereotype is that configuration management people are concerned with tools and control. They are conservative, and they prefer slow, predictable progress. They are also "the few" as compared with "the many" developers in an organization. Software engineers (so the stereotype goes) are reckless. They want to build things fast, and they are confident that they can code their way out of any situation. These are extreme stereotypes, and in my experience, the good software engineers and the good release/quality assurance/configuration management people have a common goal: They are focused on delivering quality systems with the least amount of wasted effort.

Good configuration management practice is not the silver bullet to building systems on time, nor are patterns, Extreme Programming (XP), the Unified Process, or anything else that you might hear about. It is, however, a part of the toolkit that most people ignore because they fear "process," often because of bad experiences in the past (Wiegers 2002).

This book describes some common software configuration management practices. The book will be particularly interesting to software developers working in small teams who suspect that they are not using software configuration management as effectively as they can. The techniques that we describe are not tool specific. As with any set of patterns or best practices, the ease with which you can apply the patterns may depend on whether your tool explicitly supports them.

## WHY I WROTE THIS BOOK

I started my software development career with a small R&D group based in the Boston area. Aside from the many interesting technical problems we encountered as part of our jobs, we had the added twist of having joint development projects with a group in our parent company's home base in Rochester, New York. This experience helped me recognize early in my career that software development wasn't just about good design and good coding practices but also about coordination among people in the same group and even teams in different cities. Our group took the lead in setting up the mechanics of how we would share code and other artifacts of the development process. We used the usual things to make working together easier, such as meetings, teleconferences, and e-mail lists. The way we set up our (and the remote team's) software configuration management system to share code played a very large part in making our collaboration easier.

The people who set up the SCM process for our Boston group used techniques that seemed to have been tried throughout their careers. As I moved on to other organizations, I was amazed to find how many places were struggling with the same common problems—problems that I knew had good solutions. This was particularly true because I had been with a number of start-ups that were only one or two years old when I joined. One to two years is often the stage in a start-up where you are hiring enough people that coordination and shared vision are difficult goals to attain.

A few years into my career, I discovered patterns. Erich Gamma, Richard Helm, Ralph Johnson, and John Vlissides were just finishing the book *Design Patterns* (Gamma et al. 1995), and the Hillside Group was organizing the first Pattern Languages of Programs (PLoP) conference. There is a lot of power in the idea of patterns because they are about using the right solution at the right time and because patterns are interdisciplinary; they are not just about domain- or language-specific coding techniques but about how to build software from all perspectives, from the code to the team. I presented a number of papers in workshops at the various PLoP conferences that dealt with patterns at the intersection of design, coding, and configuration management (Berczuk 1995, 1996a, 1996b; Appleton et al. 1998; Cabrera et al. 1999; Berczuk and Appleton 2000).

At one PLoP conference, I met Brad Appleton, who is more an SCM expert than I am. We coauthored a paper about branching patterns (Appleton et al. 1998), just one aspect of SCM. After much encouragement from our peers, we started working on this book.

I hope that this book helps you avoid some common mistakes, either by making you aware of these approaches or by providing you with documentation you can use to explain methods that you already know about to others in your organization.

## WHO SHOULD READ THIS BOOK

I hope that anyone who builds software and uses a configuration management system can learn from this book. The details of the configuration management problem change depending on the types of systems that you are building, the size of the teams, and the environment that you work in. Because it's probably impossible to write a book that will address everyone's needs and keep everyone's interest, I had to limit what I was talking about. This book will be most valuable to someone who is building software, or managing a software project, in a small to medium-size organization where there is not a lot of defined process. If you are in a small company, a start-up, or a small project team in a larger organization, you will benefit most from the lessons in this book. Even if your organization has a very well-defined, heavy process that seems to be impeding progress, you'll be able to use the patterns in this book to focus better on some of the key tasks of SCM.

## HOW TO READ THIS BOOK

The introduction explains some basic concepts of software configuration management and the notation that the diagrams use. Part I provides background information about SCM and patterns. Chapter 1 introduces the software configuration management concepts used in this book. Chapter 2 talks about some of the forces that influence the decisions you make about what sort of SCM environment you have. Chapter 3 introduces the concept of patterns and the patterns in this book and how they relate to each other. Part II consists of patterns that illustrate problems and solutions to common SCM problems. Chapters 1 and 2 also define the general problems that this book addresses. To understand the how patterns fit together, you should read Chapter 3 to get an overview of the language.

After you have read the first three chapters, you can browse the patterns in Part II, starting with one you find interesting and following with ones that relate to your problem. Another approach is to read the patterns in order and form a mental picture of the connections between them.

The references to the other patterns in the book appear in the introductory paragraph for each chapter and in the Unresolved Issues section at the end of each chapter, using a presentation like this: *Active Development Line (5)*. The number in parentheses is the chapter number that contains the pattern.

Because this is a large field to cover, some of the context and Unresolved Issues sections don't refer to other patterns, either in the book or elsewhere, because they haven't been documented as of this writing. In this case, you will see a description about what a pattern might cover.

## ORIGINS OF THIS MATERIAL

Much of the material in this book has its origins in papers written for various Pattern Languages of Programs conferences by me, Brad Appleton, Ralph Cabrera, and Robert Orenstein. The patterns have been greatly revised from the original material, but it's appropriate to mention these papers to acknowledge the roles of others in this work: "Streamed Lines: Branching Patterns for Parallel Software Development" (Appleton et al. 1998), "Software Reconstruction: Patterns for Reproducing the Build" (Cabrera et al. 1999), "Configuration Management Patterns" (Berczuk 1996b).

## ABOUT THE PHOTOS

The photos that start all but two chapters are from the the Library of Congress. All the photos are from the first half of the twentieth century. With the exception of two photos (the photos for *Active Development Line (5)* and *Private System Build (8)*), they are from the collection *Depression Era to World War II ~ FSA/OWI ~ Photographs ~ 1935–1945: America from the Great Depression to World War II: Photographs from the FSA and OWI, ca. 1935–1945.* I chose these pictures because I wanted to provide a visual metaphor for the patterns. Software is an abstract concept, but many of the problems we solve, particularly the ones about teams, are similar to real-world problems. Also, I have always had an interest in photography and history.

—Steve Berczuk,
   Arlington, Massachusetts, June 2002
   steve@berczuk.com
   http://www.berczuk.com

# Contributor's Preface

## WHY I COWROTE THIS BOOK WITH STEVE

I began my software development career in 1987 as a part-time software tools developer to pay for my last year of college. Somehow it "stuck" because I've been doing some form of tool development ever since (particularly SCM tools), even when it wasn't my primary job. I even worked (briefly) for a commercial SCM tool vendor, and part of my job was to stay current on the competition. So I amassed as much knowledge as I could about other SCM tools on the market. Even after I changed jobs, I continued my SCM pursuits and frequented various tool user groups on the Internet.

At one time, I longed to advance the state of the art in SCM environments and kept up with all the latest research. I soon became frustrated with the vast gap between the "state of the art" and the "state of the practice." I concluded that I could do more good by helping advance the state of the practice to use available tools better. Not long after that, I discovered software patterns and the patterns community. It was clear that these folks were onto something important in their combination of analysis and storytelling for disseminating recurring best practices of software design.

At the time, hardly anyone in the design patterns community was attempting to write SCM patterns. SCM is, after all, the "plumbing of software development" to a lot of programmers: Everyone acknowledges that they need it, but no one wants to have to dive into it too deeply and get their hands entrenched in it. They just want it to work and not to have to bother with it all that much.

It didn't take long for me to hook up with Steve Berczuk. We wrote several SCM patterns papers together (with Ralph Cabrera) as part of my ACME project at http://acme.bradapp.net/ and later decided to work on this book. We hope this small but cohesive set of core patterns about integration and teamwork helps the unsuspecting developer-cum-project-lead survive and thrive in successfully leading and coordinating their team's collaborative efforts and integrating the results into working software.

Thank you to my wife, Maria, for her unending love and support (and for our daughter, Kaeley) and to my parents for their encouragement. Thanks also to my former manager, Arbela, for her encouragement, support, and friendship.

—Brad Appleton
   Arlington Heights, Illinois, June 2002
   brad@bradapp.net
   http://www.bradapp.net

# Acknowledgments

If you have ever read acknowledgments pages, you know it takes many more people than just the authors to produce a book. While I knew this, working on this—my first book—drove the point home very clearly. I'd like to thank our editor, Debbie Lafferty, for her patience and enthusiasm in guiding us through the process of writing our first book. I also give thanks to Deborah English, the copy editor, whose thoroughness and skill helped me express the ideas in this book better than I thought possible. I would also like to thank some of the other people at Addison-Wesley who made the book possible by attending to the large amount of work that happens after the words are written down: Amy Fleischer, our production editor; Karin Hansen, who designed the cover; Dede Cummings, who designed the text of the book and was very patient with our requests to see variations on her design; Reuben Kantor, the compositor; Barbara Ames, the proofreader; Nancy Fulton, the indexer; and Chris Guzikowski and Kate Saliba, who handled all things marketing.

I also thank everyone who provided feedback on the manuscript, including Heini Aarela, Hisham Alzanoon, Bruce Angstadt, Stanley Barton, David Bellagio, Phil Brooks, Kyle Brown, Frank Buschmann, Dave Thomas, Bernard Farrell, Linda Fernandez, Jeff Fischer, William Hasling, Kirk Knoernschild, Dmitri Lapyguine, McDonald Michael, James Noble, Damon Poole, Linda Rising, Alan Shalloway, Eric Shaver, Michael Sheetz, Dave Spring, Marianne Tromp, Bob Ventimiglia, Ross Wetmore, and Farrero Xavier Verges.

# Introduction

This introduction describes some of the basic concepts, notation, and terminology we use in this book. The vocabulary of software configuration management (SCM) is used in various ways in different contexts, and the definitions here are not a comprehensive survey of the ways these terms are used. Where possible, we use common terminology. We also provide a basic introduction to the practices of version control and some suggestions for further reading.

## KEY CONCEPTS AND TERMINOLOGY

*Software configuration management* comprises factors such as configuration identification, configuration control, status accounting, review, build management, process management, and teamwork (Dart 1992). SCM practices taken as a whole define how an organization builds and releases products and identifies and tracks changes. This book concerns itself with the aspects of SCM that have a direct impact on the day-to-day work of the people writing code and implementing features and changes to that code.

Some of the concepts that developers deal with implicitly, if not by name, are *workspaces*, *codelines*, and *integration*.

A *workspace* is a place where a developer keeps all the artifacts he or she needs to accomplish a task. In concrete terms, a workspace can be a directory tree on disk in the developer's working area, or it can be a collection of files maintained in an abstract space by a tool. A workspace is normally associated with particular versions of these artifacts. A workspace also should have a mechanism for constructing executable artifacts from its contents. For example, if you were developing in Java, your workspace would include

- Source code (.java files) arranged in the appropriate package structure

- Source code for tests

- Java library files (.jar files)

- Library files for native interfaces that you do not build (for example, .dll files in windows)

- Scripts that define how you build .java files into an executable

Sometimes a workspace is managed in the context of an integrated development environment (IDE). A workspace is also associated with one or more codelines.

A *codeline* is a progression of the set of source files and other artifacts that make up some software component as it changes over time. Every time you change a file or other artifact in the version control system, you create a *revision* of that artifact. A codeline contains every version of every artifact along one evolutionary path.

At any point in time, a snapshot of the codeline will contain various revisions of each component in the codeline. Figure I–1 illustrates this; at one point you have version 1 of both file1.java and file2.java. The next time there is a change to the codeline, the resulting state of the *tip* of the codeline comprises revision 1 of file1.java and revision 2 of file2.java. Any snapshot of the codeline that contains a collection of revisions of every component in the codeline is a *configuration* of the codeline.[1] Any configuration that is given a distinct name or number is a *version* of the codeline. If you choose to identify or mark a version as special, you define a *label*. You might label the set of revisions that went into a release, for example.

In the simplest case, you might have just one codeline that includes all your product code. Components of a codeline evolve at their own rate and have revisions that we can identify. You can identify a version of the codeline

---

1. In general, you can also "tag" different revisions of components to identify a version of the codeline—for example, version 1 of file2.java and version 3 of file1.java. But there are other, more intuitive ways of identifying a configuration like this.

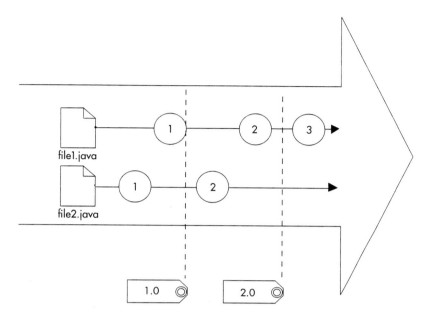

FIGURE I–1. A codeline and its components

by a label. The version of the codeline is a snapshot that includes the revisions of the components up to the point of the label.

More than one codeline can contribute to a product if each codeline consists of a coherent set of work. Each codeline can have a different purpose, and you can populate your workspace from an identifiable configuration of snapshots from various codelines. For example, you can have third-party code in one codeline, active development in another, and internal tools that are treated as internal products in a third. Figure I–2 illustrates this. Each codeline also has a *policy* associated with it. These policies define the purpose of the codeline and rules for when and how you can make changes.

As codelines evolve, you may discover that some work is derivative from the intention of the codeline. In this case, you may want to branch the file so that it can evolve independently of the original development. A *branch* of a file is revision of the file that uses the trunk version as a starting point and evolves independently. Figure I–3 illustrates this. After the second revision, someone

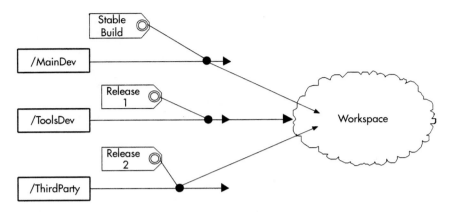

FIGURE I–2.  Populating a workspace from different codelines

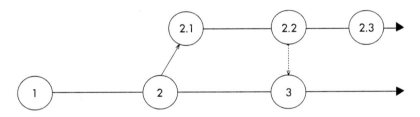

FIGURE I–3.  Branching a single file and merging with the trunk

creates a branch and changes the file through revisions 2.1, 2.2, and so on. A common notation is to indicate a branch by adding a minor version number (after a ".") to indicate that the branched revision is based on the major revision on the trunk. An example of a reason to create a branch would be that you want to start work on a new release of a product yet still be able to fix problems with the released version. In this case, you can create a branch to represent the released version and do your ongoing work on the trunk. Some of the changes you make on the branch also may need to make their way to the trunk, so you do a *merge* to integrate the changes from the branch to the trunk. Figure I–3 shows this with the dotted line from revision 2.2 to revision 3.

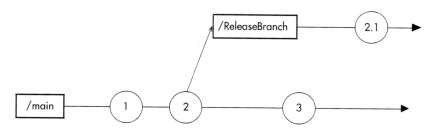

FIGURE I–4. Branching an entire codeline

Merging can be automated to some degree by tools that identify contextual text differences, but you often need to understand the intention of the change to merge correctly.

Often you will want to branch not just a single file but an associated set of files in an entire codeline. In this case, the versions refer to versions of the entire codeline taken as a unit, where a version of the codeline includes all the revisions in the codeline at that point in time, as shown in Figure I–4.

Every time you change anything in the codeline, you create a new configuration of the tip of the codeline. This new snapshot of the codeline may conceptually imply a new version to identify. In reality, most users of the code base don't need to mark each such change by a unique version number (just the noteworthy ones). Certain versions are significant, including points at which there is a product release, a branch, or a validated build. These versions of the codeline can be identified by *labels*.

## CODELINE AND BRANCHING DIAGRAMS

The discussion up to this point has illustrated the concepts of codelines, branches, and so on using the notation that this book uses for most of the examples. This section summarizes the notation and defines the symbols a bit more strictly. The codeline diagram notation is based on the notation for Unified Modeling Language (UML) sequence diagrams, with the addition of symbols to indicate versions and revisions and with the variation that the flow goes from left to right as time increases. The notation is based on the one used in the paper "Streamed Lines" (Appleton et al. 1998) and was further inspired by the diagrams in Michael Bays's book *Software Release Methodology* (Bays 1999). As with any notation, the purpose of this notation is to convey meaning clearly, so some of the diagrams in the book may use additional symbols or vary slightly from the description here where it helps to explain the subject matter.

Figure I–5 shows the notation that we use in the codeline diagrams in this book, and Table I–1 describes the symbols used.

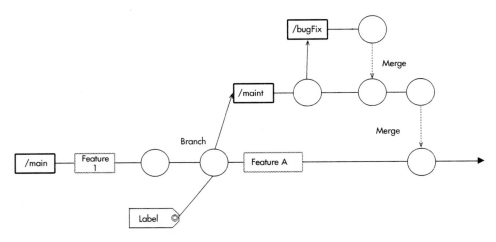

FIGURE I–5. Codeline diagram notation

## Table I-1. Codeline Diagram Notation Symbols

| Symbol | Description and Notes |
| --- | --- |
| /branch | A rectangle with a bold border is the start of a codeline. It often has an identifying name. |
| 1.0 | A circle is a version of the codeline or a revision of a file. A branch or merge point is also considered a version. It sometimes has an identifier for the branch, such as a version number. This can be blank. |

**Table I-1. Codeline Diagram Notation Symbols**

| Symbol | Description and Notes |
|---|---|
| | A gray-bordered rectangle within a codeline indicates a change task, which can be identified by a description inside the box. |
| | An arrow with a dotted line indicates a merge from the codeline at the start of the line to the codeline with the arrowhead.<br><br>A solid arrow indicates a branch. |
| | A document symbol, when it is attached to a codeline start, indicates the policy. You may also see this symbol used informally to represent a document. |
| Label | This symbol indicates a label, or an identified revision. There will be a line going from the tag to the part of the codeline that is indicated. |

## FURTHER READING

- Tichy's paper on RCS, "A System for Version Control" (Tichy 1985), is a classic paper on an early popular version control system.

- The paper, "High-Level Best Practices in Software Configuration Management" (Wingerd and Seiwald 1998), provides a good overview.

- Michael Bays's book, *Software Release Methodology* (Bays 1999), has excellent descriptions of the concepts of codelines and version control.

- Babich's book, *Software Configuration Management: Coordination for Team Productivity*, is a classic (Babich 1986).

- *Open Source Development with CVS* (Fogel and Bar 2001) provides good advice on how to use a common open source version control tool, CVS, on open source projects, among other uses.

- *Antipatterns and Patterns in Software Configuration Management* (Brown et al. 1999) has a good collection of advice on what to do and what not to do.

- *Configuration Management Principles and Practice* (Hass 2003) explains the details of configuration management practices.

- Appendixes A and B provide further sources on SCM and tools.

# Part I

## Background

*1*

# Putting a System
# Together

*Barn erection. View of roofing operation from beneath, showing construction of the roof system. Southeast Missouri Farms Project.*

*Photo by Russell Lee, May 1938. Library of Congress, Prints & Photographs Division, FSA-OWI Collection, Reproduction Number: LC-USF33-011474-M3 DLC.*

For software configuration management (SCM) to help you work effectively as a team, you must understand how all the parts of the development environment interact with each other and how SCM techniques fit into the larger picture of a software development effort. You use version control regularly, if not daily, and using it properly can speed your development effort and give you the flexibility you need to work effectively. If you use it incorrectly, it will slow you down. This chapter describes the role that good software configuration management practice can play in a productive development environment.

## BALANCING STABILITY AND PROGRESS

Any complex piece of software is the product of a team of people who need to work together. They must coordinate ideas and code so that each team member can make progress without interfering with the work of other people on the team. For example, you might make a code change that implements a feature that you are responsible for, but if you don't communicate or coordinate with the rest of the team, you may break some other team members' code unexpectedly.

Some development organizations take one of these extreme positions.

- Speed is essential, so we will worry about quality and versioning later. Besides, we're small enough that everyone knows what everyone else is doing.

- Quality is essential. We will work slowly, following processes to the letter, regardless of how it frustrates people on the project or reduces productivity. We work on one release at a time.

## GLACIAL DEVELOPMENT

One of the most common issues I see between release engineering and the development organization has to do with finishing a release. Typically, this is done with a "code freeze," which is a period of time when access to the current codeline in the version control system is restricted so that only critical changes are made to the code. Because there is a risk that anyone can add a destabilizing change at any time, a code freeze makes a certain amount of sense from the point of view of those who want to ensure that they know what they are releasing as a product. The conflict comes when the developers have work to do for later releases at the same time.

If the codeline is frozen for too long (days or weeks), either development stops or developers resort to "unsafe" practices, such as trading files to share code (instead of using the version control system) or making lots of changes between check-ins, making it harder to back out a change later. These things hurt quality and stability too, but it's not as visible a problem. One can avoid many of these problems with a good understanding of both the issues and how to use the tools.

So, if long code freezes are a problem, why do they persist? They persist because people are not using their tools well. You can avoid a code freeze with judicious branching. This assumes that the code is ready for a freeze. A too aggressive precheck-in validation requirement can lead people to start copying files instead of using the version control system. These are situations where the version control discipline has broken down, and version control doesn't fit in with the way people work and the way they waste time. This frustrates the individual developer and will eventually frustrate management when release dates slip (because of slow progress) or morale declines (because of extra time that people put in to compensate for the slow progress). This often occurs because version control processes and tools are put in place before the organization understands how people work and how the product is structured. Some procedures make sense for every environment. But for most other cases, the techniques must meet the needs of the team.               *continued*

Because developers are creative people, they often find ways to work around processes that do not work. Here is another statement that some may find controversial: Version control is a supporting discipline. Developers need to work with version control and release management tools and techniques because it is essential to track what they are developing. But version control should support the developers' work style. Because developers are smart, they will use techniques that help them get their work done.

Of course, neither of these sounds entirely correct, but we follow them anyway because each sounds like a good approach, and if we have been burned by another approach in the past, following one of these philosophies may lead us to believe that we are avoiding problems we've seen in the past. Consider the number of times you have experienced one of the following situations in a software organization.

- "We're in a code freeze. No one may check in any code until the product ships." This can be a period of two days or even a week. Although this increases stability for the to-be-shipped product in a simple way, it hurts work on subsequent versions and may even hurt the viability of a product because releases take longer to start and finish.

- "Just copy the files somewhere. I'll use your version." This is faster, but it increases the risk of inconsistencies between developers and can cause confusing problems later.

- "It works for me! Do you have the correct version of the code?" Although one developer may have an environment that works, this is a symptom of undisciplined and inconsistent use of version control.

- "We use this tool in development, but builds are done with another version control tool. Be sure to keep them in sync!" This "solves" the hard problem of having a consistent tool set, but using manual steps to keep both code streams synchronized can cause errors and unpredictable builds.

## THE ROLE OF SCM IN AGILE SOFTWARE DEVELOPMENT

Agile software development approaches acknowledge the reality of change in software development and suggest that you adapt your development methods to acknowledge that some projects have high levels of uncertainty and risk. In agile approaches, "control focuses on boundaries and simple rules rather than prescriptive, detailed procedures and processes" (Highsmith 2002). Often people think of configuration management and version control as process-heavy things that might get in the way of the "real work" of coding. For many projects, SCM does get in the way, and some organizations overcompensate and don't use the tools to help them because of a fear that a process is inherently limiting. Other organizations want control and have so much process around version control that they hurt themselves. The right amount of version control is appropriate in agile projects. The approach to configuration management and version control that this book describes is most suited for agile teams, where the development pace is rapid enough that you don't want processes to get in the way, but you don't want to be stepping over each other either.

Often conflicts about software configuration management arise because of the difficulty of determining how much structure you need. Too little and chaos reigns, too much and the environment becomes stagnant. Highsmith describes how this debate is really about balancing adaptation with anticipation (Highsmith 2002). Highsmith also observes that "one of the reasons for the divide between process and practice is often the perception that an onerous process reduces the incentive to use *any* process." This reflects the reality that what matters is not your process as much as what people actually do.

A common area where the disconnect is obvious is in how a company handles branching. A company's branching model often does not match its business model. A company that wants frequent product releases may have complex branching structures and need time-intensive merges. Another company may have many customers using independent releases but have few branches, trying to manages the differences between the customer versions in some other way. This often happens because they misunderstand their tools and techniques or because they are striving for some sort of ideal model that is inappropriate for their situation.

Much of the heavyweight application of SCM techniques comes from a desire for perfection. Seeking an ideal isn't always the best approach to a successful project. As Gerald Weinberg says, "Reasonableness saves enormous amounts of time" (Weinberg 2002).

## SCM IN CONTEXT

Many good software development practices exist that current developers just don't follow, even though these practices have been around for a while, as Steve McConnell comments (McConnell 2002). Incremental integration and source code control have been around since 1980. These are two approaches that you can add to your process and get a major gain in productivity with a minimum of effort. This book shows you how.

Software configuration management processes and tools support at least two classes of tasks in the development process: management and day-to-day software development (Conradi and Westfechtel 1998). The management-related tasks that software configuration management supports include identification of product components and their versions, change control procedures, status accounting, and audit and review. For day-to-day activities, SCM helps you, as a developer, with version control functions that allow you to record the composition of versioned software products accurately as they are revised, maintain consistency between interdependent components, and build compiled code, executables, and other derived objects from their sources.

This separation between management and development activities doesn't make a lot of sense. The things developers do are necessary for the management support tasks to be meaningful; you can't identify product components if there is no product to identify. At times the SCM process—particularly the management support aspects—seems to impede development work as opposed to enhancing it. One reason for this is that the SCM processes are often defined with the goals and needs of management first and ignore the daily needs of the developers. Another is that the processes don't use the appropriate techniques, out of ignorance or a (misguided) attempt to avoid potential risks.

There are many reasons that organizations make the same mistakes in applying SCM practices and, as a result, frustrate developers and reduce productivity and quality. One reason is that some organizations lose sight of the real goal of their work. The goal of a software development organization is to develop software that solves a customer's problem and to deliver quality software. The definition of quality is important here, so we use the definition "value to some person" (Weinberg 1991).

Some organizations put a lot of energy into doing things that don't help with the process of making useful software. Some of these places talk a lot about "the customer" and "quality" and "productivity," but their actions don't always support those spoken goals. Gerald Weinberg describes this sort of situation as a lack of *congruent behavior* (Weinberg 1986). Noncongruent behavior confuses people and hurts quality.

Some organizations make decisions that have more to do with avoiding change and expense than with writing quality (and income-producing) software. Often these decisions are well intentioned; they end up being counterproductive because they are made without understanding all aspects of how developers work and without considering of how their decisions affect other parts of the development process. A team may not create a branch when a branch would appear to be helpful because the manager of the team had earlier experienced branching as being problematic. These survival rules are useful for reducing risk, but when overapplied they can increase risk. Gerald Weinberg says:

> Survival rules are not stupid; they are simply overgeneralizations of rules we once needed for survival. We don't want to simply throw them away. Survival rules can be transformed into less powerful forms, so that we can still use their wisdom without becoming incongruent (Weinberg 1993).

Although members of a team spend large amounts of time and energy thinking through how to design a software component, teams rarely put the same effort into thinking about how they work. In particular, many source control practices often don't fit the needs of all their users. Often the SCM practices are established at one point and are then continued somewhat blindly. One reason that SCM practices don't adapt to a team's needs is that some of these practices are organization wide, and it is hard to justify, not to mention implement, global change.

A reason that practices may not meet the needs of the users in the first place is that the easy target for changing the version control process is the tool, and discussions of how to work with version control often get lost in deciding what tool to get. Sometimes organizations decide that what they need is a high-end (and powerful) tool such as ClearCase. When they know they can't afford that, they decide they shouldn't get something else, and they continue to use a tool that does not meet their needs—for example, Microsoft Visual Source Safe.

## KEEPING IT SIMPLE

Sometimes processes really do help get things done in a stable and repeatable way. Everyone involved in the work needs to have the same goal and vision for a process to work. When the work styles of the release management team and the development team don't mesh, and the processes involve many manual steps, there can be glitches that slow things down.

Consider the story of the company where the developers drive the process of what is part of the product. When they want to start using a new third-party component, they release it into the repository, and everyone starts using it on the next update. The release management team, however, doesn't just build using what is in the repository but only from a well-defined list, and they don't pay attention to development announcements about updates. Invariably, a number of nightly builds will fail until the release team does them with the new version. There are a number of responses to this problem. The release manager can scold the developers, the release team can use the version control tool's reporting facilities to check for updates, or the release team can monitor the development team's announcements for updates.

Of these approaches, scolding is the least effective and often the most frequently chosen approach. Having a common approach to the version control process or using tools to remedy differences can make things run much more smoothly.

In the quest for a good solution, we often lose sight of the fact that many small-scale changes can have a large impact on how we work. Although a new tool might make a big difference, using your current tool effectively and working within its limitations also help greatly. Another reason that source control is ignored is that you can resolve most source control process issues through manual processes. Although this *is* work and has a cost, it is one that most managers don't see. As when planning for a product, you should consider the developers as a class of users for the SCM process. "People who are left out of planning invariably turn up late in a change project to haunt you" (Weinberg 1991). In this case, the "haunting" will be visible in terms of frustration and decreased productivity.

This book will help you understand some of the techniques and processes of SCM and how to apply them in a way that allows you to work more effectively. Many of the techniques can be applied incrementally and locally so that you don't need to change the entire organization to improve the way you work. It may also provide you with a means to explain how some day-to-day practices can support both your needs as a developer and the larger needs of a someone managing a product release.

## SCM AS A TEAM SUPPORT DISCIPLINE

Encompassing the management and development support aspects of SCM, configuration management, and in particular version control, plays a role in supporting the work of teams. Version control can certainly benefit a one- or two-person workgroup, but when you have more people than can comfortably manage to communicate to each other everything they are doing on a project, you need an infrastructure to support communication. A version control system is the way teams can get the answers to questions about who made recent changes, when something broke, what code customers are using, and what components are related. This is what we mean when we say that software configuration management serves as a mechanism for communication, change management, and reproducibility.

To develop software you need to do obvious things such as define requirements, develop designs, write code for the product and for tests, and write documentation. The hardest and one of the most important things that has to happen is effective communication. Communication is not just sharing status and general information but also sharing enough detailed information about what people are doing so that teams can work together and be more productive. Although engineers often spend a lot of effort on design and implementation decisions, engineers and their managers often leave teamwork issues to "just happen."

You can realize important improvement in team productivity and software quality by using the appropriate version control practices. Unfortunately, many version control practices are often established without a good consideration of the things that influence how code is written. Some of these things are as follows.

- The *structure of the organization.* A three-person team in one room has different needs than a large team spread across the globe.

- The *product architecture.* Some points in the architecture allow for more decoupling than other points.

- The *tools* available. Some tools support some techniques more effectively than other tools. If you have a tool that does not handle branching well, you may want to come up with a different release model or get a better tool.

For each of these influences you could change the factors themselves. Put your whole team in one city (or in one room); fix the product architecture to reduce coupling; buy a "better" SCM tool. These changes can be expensive. It can also be expensive (though not as obviously) *not* to fix the other problems. We often find that the costs of changing a tool, for example, are very visible, but the costs (in productivity, morale, and so on) of using the wrong tool badly are hidden. It may be easier to adapt the way you use version control to the way people work than to change the environment. Chapter 2 discusses the role of organizations and teams in more detail.

Our goal in this book is to point out the solutions that are effective, given the environment you must work in. You may be surprised by the improvements you can find by making small changes in process. You will also identify aspects of your environment that you should change. In the end, we want to help you build better software faster, not force you to use a particular process.

Some of the techniques are things that affect how the team works and may need consensus or management buy-in. Some are practices that you and one or two colleagues can do on your own.

There are many aspects to team communication, including organizations or management. These things do need to be considered because they have an impact on how people work. This book is about the tools and techniques you can use as a person developing software to work cooperatively with members of your team and members of other teams. The way teams communicate their work products to each other is through their software configuration management and version control practices.

## WHAT SOFTWARE CONFIGURATION MANAGEMENT IS

Like many things in our discipline of software development, software configuration management means many things to many people. This section discusses some dimensions of SCM and highlights the aspects we are concerned with.

SCM serves at least two distinct purposes: management support and development support.

A standard definition of software configuration management includes the following aspects (Dart 1992).

- *Configuration identification*—determining which body of source code you are working with. This makes it possible to know, among other things, that you are fixing a bug in the source code that is in the correct release.

- *Configuration control*—controlling the release of a product and changes to it throughout the lifecycle to ensure consistent creation of a baseline software product. This can include not only changes to source files but also which compiler and other tools were used, so issues such as differences between compiler support for language features can be taken into account.

- *Status accounting audit*—recording and reporting the status of components and change requests and gathering vital statistics about components in the product. One question we may want to answer is, How many files were affected by fixing this one bug?

- *Review*—validating the completeness of a product and maintaining consistency among the components by ensuring that components are in an appropriate state throughout the entire project lifecycle and that the product is a well-defined collection of components.

- *Build management*—managing what processes and tools developers use to create a build or release, so it can be repeated.

- *Process management*—ensuring that the organization's development processes are followed by those developing and releasing the software.

- *Teamwork*—controlling the interactions of all the developers working together on a product so that people's changes are inserted into the system in a timely fashion.

Ideally, a configuration management process should both serve broad organizational interests and make the work of a developer easier. A good SCM process makes it possible for developers to work together on a project effectively, both as individuals and as members of a team. Although various tools can make the process simpler, tools alone are not enough. Successful development organizations also use certain patterns for software configuration management .

With respect to team interactions, a successful configuration management process enables the following.

- Developers can work together on a project, sharing common code. For example, a developer of a derived class needs to stay in sync with whoever is developing a base class, and a client of a class needs to be able to work with the current version of that class.

- Developers can share development effort on a module, such as a class or simply a single source file. This can be by design or to allow someone to fix a bug in another person's module if the other person is unavailable.

- Developers can access the current stable (tested) version of a system so they can check whether their code will work when someone else tries to integrate it into the current code set.

- Developers can back up to a previous stable version of a system so they can test their code against the prior consistent versions of the system to track down problems.

- Developers can checkpoint changes to a module and back up to a previous version of that module. This facility makes it safer to experiment with a major change to a module that is basically working.

Attaining all these goals involves compromises. A cynic could paraphrase Otto von Bismarck's remark, "To retain respect for sausages and laws, one must not watch them in the making," to apply to software systems and processes. We need to watch how our processes evolve and attend to what works and what does not work, and by leveraging the experiences of others, we can improve.

Version control is an important part of making team software development work effectively. Version control practices help people work on the same components in parallel without interfering with each other's work. Software configuration management and version control practices allow you to do things such as the following:

- Develop the next version of a piece of software while fixing problems with the current one

- Share code with other team members in a controlled way, allowing you to develop code in parallel with others and join with the current state of the codeline

- Identify what versions of code went into a particular component

- Analyze where a change happened in the history of a component's development

The next section identifies in a development project some of the tensions that interfere with establishing good SCM practice.

## THE ROLE OF TOOLS

The first question people ask when they talk about version control is, What tool are you using? This is a practical question that reveals the important impact tools have on the way we work.

Although the tool influences how you work, it should not be the main concern. Of course, tools with a feature set that matches your needs make things work better. But the most important thing is to balance the capabilities of the tool with the needs of the organization and the developers. It is critical to make the processes easy so that people will follow them. Another aspect that this book shares with advocates of agile development is that it is the people on a team and what they do that is important, or as the Agile Manifesto says, "Individuals and interactions are more important than processes and tools."

When you find that an everyday practice needs a large number of (hard to remember) manual steps, you may want to question the capabilities of the tool or the value of the practice.

Appendix B describes some common tools and how to use them to implement the patterns using the concepts of the tools. Appendix A provides even more information on SCM resources.

## THE LARGER WHOLE

Tools, product architecture, and organization are all important aspects of the software development environment that we need to take into account when building software systems, but when we let them drive the process at the expense of delivering quality software in a reliable manner, we get into trouble. There is a lot to do besides coding—documentation and testing are part of the process, and quality and reproducibility are things that help get a product out. The next chapter discusses in more detail the other pieces of the picture and how SCM fits into this picture.

## THIS BOOK'S APPROACH

This book approaches the problem of using software configuration management and version control by looking at the overall environment within which you use version control and by demonstrating how to solve problems after considering your specific environment.

This book places a number of well-documented best practices in the context of a team's work style and the constraints of your organization. This book does not present a set of rules you should follow but a set of practices that work together (with variations).

The practices are cast as patterns. We discuss patterns in general in Chapter 3. You don't need to understand patterns to use the ideas in this book, although you may get an added benefit if you do.

## UNRESOLVED ISSUES

How do we improve the way we use version control? The next chapter describes how a pattern-oriented approach is helpful.

## FURTHER READING

This book is not about software architecture or process per se, so we cannot go into as much detail about these issues as we would like. The following references provide more detail.

- Garlan and Shaw give a good overview of architectural styles (Shaw and Garlan 1996).

- The *Pattern-Oriented Software Architecture* series describes a number of architectural patterns (Schmidt et al. 2000; Buschmann et al. 1996).

- *The Unified Modeling Language User Guide* discusses the various architectural views suggested by the Unified Process (Booch et al. 1999).

- Jim Highsmith provides a good overview of the current set of agile techniques in his book *Agile Software Development Ecosystems* (Highsmith 2002).

An important aspect of improving processes is detecting the problems in an organization and influencing people to change.

- *Seeing Systems: Unlocking the Mysteries of Organizational Life*, by Barry Oshry (Oshry 1996), is a useful and entertaining book about how to detect cycles of behavior that need to change and how to change them.

- *Getting to Yes* (Fisher et al. 1991) is a classic book on negotiation, and informal negotiation is something that you may find yourself doing when you try to make changes in the way people work. *Getting Past No* (Ury 1993) is also worth reading.

- *Becoming a Technical Leader*, by Gerald Weinberg (Weinberg 1986), has great advice on leading from any role.

# 2

# The Software Environment

*Elevated structure and buildings, Lower Manhattan, New York, December 1941.*

*Photo by Arthur Rothstein. Library of Congress, Prints & Photographs Division, FSA-OWI Collection, Reproduction Number: LC-USF34-024346-D.*

To use software configuration management (SCM) properly, you need to understand how its techniques fit into the larger picture. This chapter discusses some of the other aspects of the development environment and the processes we use to create and maintain them so that we can understand how SCM fits in.

## GENERAL PRINCIPLES

By software configuration management, we mean the set of processes that one uses to create and maintain a consistent set of software components to release. Version control is the part of the SCM process that a developer sees most often. It manifests itself through your version control tool and how you use it. Often you associate the use of a tool with a set of policies or rules for how to use it to follow the lifecycle the organization needs (check-ins, builds, releases, and so on). Sometimes the policies are enforced automatically; other times developers must follow a manual procedure.

We can't give you one set of rules to say how to use version control or which tool to use. How to use it (or any other tool or technique) depends strongly on your situation. Just as you might use different tools for building a doghouse as opposed to a summer vacation cottage, different software project teams need different approaches. If you use big complicated tools for a small project where everyone communicates well, you may slow things down and increase costs. Likewise, trying blindly to apply techniques that worked well in an initial product release project in a five-person start-up may cause trouble in the same start-up six months later with 20 people working on release 3 (and maintaining release 2 and release 1).

20

Working in a team adds a need for communication and changes the way you would execute these principles. For a one-person project, you can try to build your software system and accompanying development environment based solely on first principles of "good" coding practice. Some basic version control system will help you with your memory, but you should not (usually) have any communication issues. Once more than one person is involved in building the system, communication and interaction between developers come into play. Each software system is built in a context that shapes the code and the patterns of work. The same principles you use as an individual developer also apply when you work as part of a team. Each team and every project are different, so no one process will work. Version control is a core part of the communication mechanism. You need to vary the details of how you use version control based on your situation. To do that, you need to step back and look at the places where software is built.

We can apply a few general principles to using configuration management on any software project. The details of how to apply the principles vary, depending on the size and nature of the team. Some of these principles are as follows.

- Use *version control*. Version control is the backplane on which software organizations communicate work products among themselves. This sounds obvious, but some organizations do not track versions. Even if they have a version control tool, they do not use it. They copy files between developers without checking them in. They have no way of identifying what went into a release and how to reproduce the system at a point in time. Some places need more lightweight tools and processes than others, and some development techniques allow for more flexibility in the process, but every team needs to have a way to do version control and needs to use it to communicate code changes among the members.

- Do *periodic builds*, and integrate frequently. Have some sort of periodic build process that builds what looks like the current version of the software so that people can see how well things fit together. The longer you put off integration, the harder integration problems will be. How often you need to do this depends on a number of details about your organization. Extreme Programming (Beck 2000) and other agile approaches say to integrate continuously, but for simple systems, that may add too much overhead. Erring on the side of integrating too often is generally better, but integration takes time, and you want to find the point where integrating more often speeds up the overall process.

- Allow for *autonomous work*. Every team, even those with one person, may need to work on various points in time of the codeline. Team members should be able to control what versions of what components they are working on. Sharing "common" components may work well most days, but when you need to diverge from working on the latest code, it will probably be for an emergency.

- Use *tools*. If you have too many manual processes, people may make mistakes or simply skip a step out of frustration or perceived need. Be lazy and write tools.

How you apply these general rules depends on the environment you are building your software in. And you need to apply other software engineering practices to testing, coding, and related issues. See the Further Reading section for pointers. The next sections describe some elements of the software environment.

## WHAT SOFTWARE IS ABOUT

In its most concrete form, a software system is the sum of all of its code. You write code, and you end up with an application that does something useful. Other artifacts also make the system run: data, documentation, and anything else you need for your system. The code, however, defines the shape of the other artifacts. Without the code or these artifacts, there is nothing to deliver to a customer or user.

To understand how you build a software system, you need to think about more than just the code and other physical artifacts. You need to understand how the people on the team work, how the product is structured, and what the goals and structure of the organization are. We often ignore social issues such as organizational structure and politics, thinking them secondary to what we perceive to be the main goal: building a software system. Although this sounds appealing (focusing on the core goals and all that), these other factors are important to consider. If you don't consider them, they will get in the way when you try to build and deliver systems quickly.

It's easy to get lost in all the other factors. Corporate politics alone can cause you to spin endlessly. One way to think about the software environment where you are using configuration management is to model it as consisting of the following structures.

- Where the developer codes: the *workspace*. This is the day-to-day code environment of the developers.

- Where the coding takes place: the *organization*. The developer works in the context of an organizational structure. Teams are developing software, testing, marketing, doing customer support, and so on.

- Where the code fits in: the *product architecture*. Related to the product architecture is the release structure, which specifies how many releases are being developed together.

- Where the code (and code history) is kept: the *configuration management environment*. This includes tools, processes, and policies.

These structures all have associated with them policies and processes that sustain them. Although it's not always obvious, these structures influence each other (see Figure 2–1), and if you don't take the influences into account, your work may be harder than it needs to be.

## POLICIES INFLUENCING WORK

One company I worked at had a very rigorous precheck-in testing regime that developers had to follow. You had to run a very long suite of tests—approximately 30 minutes—before checking in any code.

In the lifecycle of this company, 30 minutes was a long time, so people worked to avoid the long tests by either checking in less often, which meant that a check-in would add more than one feature or would fix more than one bug, or skipping the tests, which hurt the reliability of the code base. There are more extreme examples of policies affecting work. The developers eventually lobbied for a precheck-in smoke test that took a couple of minutes to run, and the processes got back in sync with good work practices.

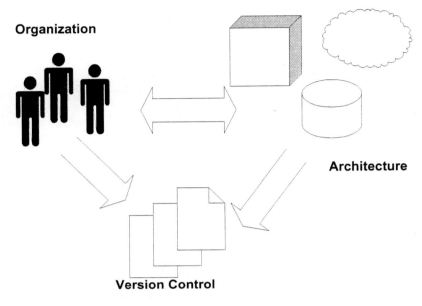

FIGURE 2–1.  The interactions between elements of the environment

Some examples of these influences follow.

- The organization influences the structure of the code and the architecture (Conway's Law).

- The organization and the architecture both influence version control policies. A less tightly coupled architecture can be developed in parallel more easily than a tightly coupled one. A small team in one room can communicate more effectively than a large team spread across the globe. In each case, version control policies can compensate.

- The version control environment and the organization influence the structure and use of workspaces. You can use some policies to alter the way people work; this isn't always the best way to do things because it is working backward in many cases, but it can have an influence.

Often tools and mechanisms for work style and version control fail because they are applied without understanding the reality that the mechanisms need to work well with the existing environment.

The next sections discuss each of the development structures and its interactions in more detail.

## THE DEVELOPMENT WORKSPACE

Software development happens in the workspaces of the developers in the team. A workspace is simply the set of components a developer is currently working with, including source code the developer is editing and using for reference, build components necessary to run the software, and third-party components. The *Private Workspace (6)* pattern discusses the components of a workspace in more detail.

Each developer has one or more workspaces, depending on the number of projects the developer is working on. The build team may also have an integration workspace in which to do periodic builds.

## ARCHITECTURE

"Software architecture" is a widely used and widely misunderstood term. It can mean many things, depending on the person using the term and the audience. Sometimes different understandings of what "architecture" means can lead to legal disputes. Steve McConnell recounts a story about being an expert witness in a case where a company sued a VP over nonperformance of work duties, in part because they had a different understanding of what an architecture was (McConnell 2000).

The one thing that most definitions have in common is that the architecture defines some aspects of the structure of the system. IEEE Std. 610.12 defines architecture as "The organizational structure of a system of components." The architecture places constraints on where and how parts fit together and how easy it is to change or add functionality. Even if there is no explicit architecture document or architectural vision, there is an implicit "architecture" that the existing body of code defines. The code establishes a structure you need to work within, perhaps changing it as you go. Even in a "green fields" development project, there are still "architecture" decisions that constrain software decisions, including (but not limited to) method of communication, programming language, and choice of database.

For the purpose of discussing team software development, we define architecture as "a description of how the parts of the software fit together that provides guidance about how the system should be modified." This includes both the logical and physical structure of the system, including relationships between components, deployment units, and even the way the code is structured in the source tree.

The role of architecture in developing a version control strategy is to establish the structure of the version control modules and therefore how we make concurrent work easier. Grinter writes that "software architectures represent another mechanism of interaction supporting collaborative work at a higher level of systems abstraction" (Grinter 1995).

The architecture influences this because the architecture defines

- What makes up a deliverable unit

- The communication paths among the units

- Indirectly the directory structure and other structural aspects of the source code respository

For example, one way to allow concurrent work is to design a system using a pipes-and-filters architecture (Buschmann et al. 1996). At a finer level of detail, you can decouple systems using patterns such as Parser-Builder (Berczuk 1996a) or Visitor (Gamma et al. 1995). These patterns each allow teams to treat the code that they own as fairly separate from other teams' code. The pipes-and-filters approach can be a way to design a system that is being built by teams a large distance from each other. It is entirely possible to structure your source tree in a way that conflicts with this goal, and, if you ignore integration process issues, the architecture alone will not save you.

An architecture comprises a number of views, each of which exposes the part of the picture that you care about in a specific context. The UML (Booch et al. 1999) takes this approach by defining the following four views as well as a *use case* view that describes what the software does (Krutchen 1995).

- *Implementation,* which defines units of work at various degrees of granularity.

- *Deployment,* which specifies where physical components are put. The deployment structure has a strong impact on how software is built.

- *Design*, which is the lower-level details. Except for the way the class design affects the module structure and the dependencies between components, this has the least effect on how the version control should be structured.

- *Process*, which affects performance, scalability, and throughput. This has the least relevance to our discussion, though it is important.

Architecture is heavily influenced by organizational structure. In certain occasions an architecture can influence the formation of an organization, but most often, the product architecture is developed in an existing organization.

Architecture can be organized with the organization in mind. The architecture may match the structure of the organization, based on location and the skill levels of developers of components.

Modularity leads to decoupling, which adds concurrency to the development process.

> Modularity is about separation: When we worry about a small set of related things, we locate them in the same place. This is how thousands of programmers can work on the same source code and make progress. We get in trouble when we use that small set of related things in lots of places without preparing or repairing them (Gabriel and Goldman 2000).

The architecture and organization affect the best way to partition source code into directories.

- The architecture/module structure. The product's module structure is the strongest influence on the source code structure. A typical partitioning is to have the source code for one module in one directory so that you can manage the files more easily. If you are using a language that has header files, such as C++, or interface definition files, such as COM, or CORBA IDL files, you may want to put these files in a common location, apart from the bulk of the source code; this makes it easier to ship interface definitions to customers if you provide an API.

- The team structure—the number of people working on a project and the number of people working on a module. Modules may be grouped logically based on the people working on them. This may not always be optimal, but it happens.

- The particulars of your development environment. Do you have symbolic links? What is your programming language?

## THE ORGANIZATION

This section discusses some of the aspects of an organization that affect the way software systems come into being. This is a large area, which has research papers (Allen 1997a, 1997b; Allen et al. 1998) and entire books (Weinberg 1991; Brooks 1975) devoted to it, so we mention only some of the more relevant factors here.

Software development is, in many respects, a social discipline. The organization can significantly influence how a product is designed and how teams are structured. Things can get difficult when your development approach conflicts with the structures the organization imposes. Changing the organizational structure is often the best, if most difficult, fix. Even if changing the organization is impossible, the real danger is in not acknowledging these influences and in focusing only on the immediate programming tasks.

Organization has an influence from the perspective of workspace structure and version control because the structure of the organization constrains communication. The organization affects communication by the *distance* between people and teams. Distance is a measure of how hard it is for teams and team members to interact. It can be about physical distance but is not always. Organizational structure divides responsibilities, which can also make communication harder if the responsibilities are not divided in a manner consistent with the needs of the application.

The organization can be more subtle in its influence on the architecture and the way you work. The nature of the organization and its culture constrain the team dynamic, the architecture, the goals of the development process, and how problems are handled.

Distance is about the following:

- Physical location. Teams that are not physically close can have a lower bandwidth of communication.

- Culture and team dynamics. An appropriate culture can result in teams that are physically far apart having very good communication and can also result in people in the same room having very poor communication.

- Organizational structures that dictate communication paths. This is an aspect of culture since communication need not follow corporate structures, but if this is an ethic in your organization, you might do well to have the architectural communication paths follow the organizational boundaries.

You need to be aware of the effects of organizational distance, and we encourage you to be a change agent to improve the long-term picture, but simply building your work structures so that they are robust in the face of these organizational issues will generate a big win.

Some other organizational influences include

- Skill sets of people

- Distance, which encompasses many things, including physical distance

- Values and culture

- Location of personnel and other resources

- Team stability

- Type of company: consulting company versus product company versus product company with customer-specific changes

The structure of an organization can have a large impact on how the software is built and hence on coordination needs. Organizational forces can have a very strong impact on the product architecture and can control process aspects such as when and how releases are created, tested, and so on. It is beyond the scope of this book to tell you how to match the product process and architecture to adapt and leverage the structure of the organization. We briefly describe some of the issues so that you can better understand them.

Although many say that an ideal development environment has developers who are near each other and who communicate effectively, many real organizations have resources that are geographically distributed, and you need to help them work well together. One way is to distribute responsibilities so that remote groups can have very well-defined interfaces between them and few dependencies. You also need to structure the version control system so that people at all locations can see all the code easily.

Some influences of organization on architecture that are particularly relevant are the following.

- Module structure (Bass et al. 1998). Modules should be developed by people who can work well together, and aspects such as geography or technology experience may dictate that certain components should be developed by certain groups. There is an interplay with the product architecture here; you may have to make the choice of assigning a component to a group with the most appropriate technical experience, for example, or a group with lesser technical skills but in a better position to interact (by whatever means are appropriate—this is not an argument for geographic proximity) with the groups that interface with its work product.

- Integration Policy: How often all of a system's components are integrated is often a function of organizational policy.

- Workspace management: How you set up your local development environment and how your workspace relates to others'.

- Version control and identification: How you use source control tools and other means to coordinate changes with others, publish your changes, and reproduce environments, such as when you need to fix a bug in an earlier release. This includes issues such as branching and labeling, which often cause much consternation.

- Coordination: How you work together with other teams and developers.

- Identification and Auditing: How you know what you built.

## THE BIG PICTURE

Given all the things that have a part in building a software system, it is easy to lose track of your primary goal, which is to build a software system. It is easy to become overwhelmed by the technologies and techniques you use as part of the process. Version control, configuration management, building, testing, pair programming, branching, and other process activities are all aspects of the software engineering environment. These techniques support the process. A goal is not to branch, for example. Branching is one way to accomplish concurrent development or isolate a line of work. This may seem like an obvious statement, but I have seen a lot of energy expended on figuring out how to accomplish tasks for which there were other, simpler ways to reach the end goal. An excellent bit of advice to keep in mind as you read this book is, "Don't mistake a solution method for a problem definition, especially if it is your own solution method" (Gause and Weinberg 1990).

Putting together all the influences of architecture, organization, and configuration management on each other, we see that the big-picture view of an SCM environment encompasses the tools and process for identifying, organizing, controlling, and tracking both the decomposition and recomposition of a software system's structure, functionality, evolution, and teamwork. An effective SCM environment is the glue between software artifacts, features, changes, and team members.

## FURTHER READING

- Steve McConnell has a few books that cover best practices for coding and teamwork—in particular, *Rapid Development* (McConnell 1996) and *Code Complete* (McConnell 1993) have some excellent guidelines.

- *The Pragmatic Programmer* (Hunt and Thomas 2000) talks about the value of using tools to automate processes and procedures.

- *The Practice of Programming* (Kernighan and Pike 1999) says quite a bit about the value of automation and tools.

- Mary Lynn Manns and Linda Rising provide some guidance on introducing new ideas in their paper, "Introducing Patterns into Organizations" (Manns and Rising 2002).

- Alistair Cockburn gives some good advice about writing use cases in *Writing Effective Use Cases* (Cockburn 2000). *Patterns for Effective Use Cases* (Adolph et al. 2003) provides a patterns-based approach to writing use cases.

- David Dikel and David Kane's book, *Software Architecture: Organizational Principles and Patterns* (Dikel et al. 2001), is an excellent source for information about what architecture is and how to use it.

# 3

# **Patterns**

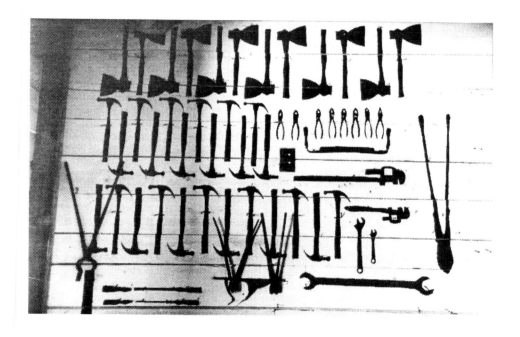

*Patterns of tools painted on wall for easy identification. Lake Dick Project, Arkansas, September 1938.*

*Photo by Russell Lee, May 1938. Library of Congress, Prints & Photographs Division, FSA-OWI Collection, Reproduction Number: LC-USF33-011692-M4.*

For configuration management to help you work effectively as a team, you must understand how all the parts of the development environment interact with each other. One way to model this is to think about the development process in terms of the relationships among the patterns in the development environment.

You do not need to master the concepts of patterns and pattern languages to find value in this book, but the pattern approach is an easy way to think about how the elements of a system work together as they compose a system. This chapter explains what patterns are and how a pattern language can help you understand and improve your team process, and it gives an overview of the patterns in the book.

## ABOUT PATTERNS AND PATTERN LANGUAGES

A solution makes sense only if you apply it at the right time. A pattern language is a way to place solutions in the context of the things you've already done.

Many books and papers talk about patterns for software, architecture, organizations and teams, and technology development, and we won't try to cover all that in this chapter. This section gives a brief overview of what patterns are about and provides references if you want more detail.

A simple definition of a pattern is a "solution to a problem in a context." Each pattern in a pattern language completes the other patterns in the pattern language. In that way, the context of a pattern is the patterns that came before it. This means that a pattern fits within other patterns to form a pattern language.

The idea of patterns and pattern languages is originally from work the architect Christopher Alexander did in building architecture to describe qualities for good architectural designs. In the 1970s he started using pattern languages to describe the events and forms that appeared in cities, towns, and buildings in the world at large.

Alexander talks about a pattern as something that "describes a problem which occurs over and over again in our environment, and then describes the core of the solution to that problem, in such a way that you can use this solution a million times over, without ever doing it the same way twice"(Alexander et al. 1977). Alexander defines a pattern as "a rule which describes what you have to do to generate the entity which it defines" (Alexander 1979). Patterns, according to Alexander, are more than just solutions. They are *good* solutions.

> And there is an imperative aspect to the pattern. The pattern solves a problem. It is not merely "a" pattern, which one might or might not use on a hillside. It is a *desirable* pattern; for a person who wants to farm a hillside, and prevent it from erosion, he *must* create this pattern in order to maintain a stable and healthy world. In this sense, the pattern not only tells him how to create the pattern of terracing, if he wants to; it also tells him that it is essential for him to do so, in certain particular contexts, and that he must create this pattern there (Alexander 1979).

> Alexander's patterns set out to be more than just cookbook solutions.

> But when properly expressed, a pattern defines an invariant field which captures all the possible solutions to the problem given, in the stated range of contexts (Alexander 1979).

> A pattern is a rule for resolving forces, but the important thing is that it fits in with other patterns.

> We see, in summary, that every pattern we define must be formulated in the form of a rule which establishes a relationship between a context, a system of forces which arise in that context, and a configuration which allows these forces to resolve themselves in that context (Alexander 1979).

Alexander's pattern language is "a system which allows its users to create an infinite variety of those . . . combinations of patterns which we call buildings, gardens, and towns" (Alexander 1979). Alexander documents patterns that exist in our towns and buildings. For example, one of Alexander's patterns is *Half Private Office*, which describes how to achieve the right balance between privacy and connection to office work.

Alexander's pattern languages are very ambitious, and the pattern language he has authored can give you much insight into architecture and urban planning. It was also the inspiration for the patterns in software.

## PATTERNS IN SOFTWARE

Although the initial work about patterns was about building things on a human scale, we can apply the basic ideas of patterns to software development. Using and writing patterns is about the quest for objective quality. Software development involves people working together to build things. These things are often similar to other things that were built in the past. In some software development organizations, the process works well because the teams apply techniques that work and cast aside techniques that do not. In other organizations they don't, so there must be something we can learn from the successes and when to apply the techniques that worked.

The first major work in software patterns was the book, *Design Patterns* (Gamma et al. 1995). This book catalogs some key techniques in object-oriented (OO) design with very good descriptions about when and how to implement them. *Design Patterns* does not capture the full power of patterns because each pattern stands by itself, and you still need a good understanding about software systems to put them together to build something larger. To help people apply design patterns, books have been written to show how to implement these patterns in various situations (Vlissides 1998) and in other languages (Alpert et al. 1998).

Other books and writings on software patterns address architecture issues (Buschmann et al. 1996; Schmidt et al. 2000) and organization issues (Coplien 1995), but the patterns are still not connected in languages. Because they are not connected, finding the correct pattern and applying it in the correct situation require a deep understanding of the patterns and the situation. Although you do need to understand something about the patterns and what you are doing to benefit from a collection of patterns, this need for finding your way through the patterns reduces a major benefit of patterns, as a way to navigate through a set of complex trade-offs and implement a good solution.

Pattern languages are useful for documenting software architecture principles, particularly object-oriented systems because of the emphasis on structure in OO systems. They can be and have been used to describe architecture systems in other paradigms. Some of the existing pattern languages and collections about software include pattern languages that describe how to build social structures such as software development organizations (Coplien 1995; Olson and Stimmel 2002) and patterns on architectural principles (Buschmann et al. 1996; Schmidt et al. 2000). The Further Reading section at the end of this chapter lists some more examples.

This book describes a pattern language that works at the intersection of the team and the architecture: the developer's workspace and its interface to the version control system. We talk about patterns that describe how people build software on a human scale. In particular, we describe patterns that people use when applying software configuration management techniques.

## CONFIGURATION MANAGEMENT PATTERNS

Patterns are a particularly useful way to think about software configuration management for the following reasons.

- SCM involves how people work in addition to the mechanics of how the code is built.

- SCM involves processes for doing things and the artifacts that result. Patterns are particularly good at describing both the process and thing aspects at the same time.

- Although there are many "best practices" for SCM, to use them effectively, you must understand how they relate to other practices you use and the environment in which you use them.

- Small local changes in SCM practices can greatly improve the process; small changes and organic growth can effect change; you don't need high-level management buy-in, although it can help.

When you think about the way the members of a team work together, some of the first words that come to mind are process and behavior. Processes and behaviors are dynamic things, and dynamic things can be hard to understand. People are better at modeling static situations and later extending the static models to include behavior. We know how to describe what a building looks like, and given a set of diagrams, we can build one that matches the specification quite nicely. We have a harder time modeling systems that have people in them. But static structures do not appear of their own accord, and they don't do anything, so you need processes to create and sustain them; this is where processes come into play. The software architecture, the way a developer's workspace is configured, and the way the SCM system is structured are all sustained by the processes you use each day.

For a team to build software consistently, you need people to implement processes consistently. There are a few ways to get that consistency. Goodwill might work, but it is better if behaviors are enforced by the tools and the environment. Sometimes this is hard to do, and you need to allow for situations that you didn't expect; otherwise, people may view the processes as arbitrary and bureaucratic rather than useful.

When there are manual procedures, you need to motivate people to follow them. People tend to follow processes more closely when they understand the rationale behind the processes. Understanding the rationale allows people to make good judgment calls when the process does not precisely cover the situation at hand. It helps to be able to explain the process in terms of the structure it supports. But passing on a complete understanding of the system takes time.

Some static things underlie all the processes that go on in a software engineering environment. Things like source code modules, executables, and version control systems are concrete things; you use a process to change things, but the process is closely tied to the other parts of the environment.

We want to take the "simple" things that we understand and then compose them to describe how to help developers work together in teams.

Using patterns is different from other ways of looking at problems because how the patterns relate to each other is as important as the problem and the solution they solve (Berczuk 1994).

Some of the patterns here may seem obvious, but the details of how to apply them are not always so obvious. This is part of their value. Alexander says that the process of applying patterns is valuable "not so much because it shows us things which we don't know, but instead, because it shows us what we know already, only daren't admit because it seems so childish, and so primitive" (Alexander 1979).

## STRUCTURE OF PATTERNS IN THIS BOOK

The patterns in this book have the following parts.

- A *title* that describes what the pattern builds.

- A *picture* that can serve as a metaphor, and perhaps as a mnemonic, for the pattern. The pictures in this book are of things in the real world of the past rather than of software or technology. We also want to emphasize that the solutions here do have analogs in the "real world"—that is, beyond software. We also hope that this approach interjects an element of humor, allowing you to remember the pattern better.

- A paragraph describing the *context* of the pattern—that is, when you should consider reading the pattern. In general, this will contain references to other patterns, some of which are in this book and others that have been published elsewhere. Because there are aspects of the team development problem that we did not cover, there may also be a prose description.

- A concise statement of the *problem* that the pattern solves.

- A detailed *problem description* illustrating the trade-offs, some dead-end solutions, and the issues that need to be resolved.

- A short summary of the *solution*.

- A description of the *solution in detail*.

- A discussion of *unresolved issues* and how to address them. This will lead you to other patterns that can address these problems.

The pattern chapters may also have a section that suggests ways to learn more about the topic of the pattern.

## THE PATTERN LANGUAGE

This section briefly describes how the patterns in this book are organized and then discusses how to use the book.

As you read through the patterns, you may find that some match your current practice, while others do not. Teamwork is a complicated thing, and a there is no simple cookbook-like approach to using the patterns in this book that will work for everyone. The best way to approach the patterns is to read through them all until you have a high-level understanding of them and then work through the patterns that are particularly relevant to you. After you have done this (or if you want to start attacking your problems now), here is one approach that we suggest starting with.

- Identify the global problem you are trying to solve. If you are reading this book, you are probably considering how to get team members to work together more efficiently.

- Look through the pattern context and problem description sections to identify the patterns you already use in your organization as well as any patterns that seem to solve pressing problems. The context sections mostly consist of other patterns in the language, but since no pattern language can be totally complete, the context of some patterns may describe a situation rather than reference patterns.

- Once you identify which patterns you already have in place, start with one of those patterns. If you are trying to establish "mainline" development, start at the first pattern in the language.

- Apply the patterns as the language directs by looking at the context and unresolved issues sections.

- Repeat this process until you have worked through the language.

Each pattern can also stand on its own to some degree.

This book shows one path through the patterns, that for doing mainline development. Parts of the language may be relevant for other situations. For example, the *Private Workspace* pattern will be useful to you regardless of the sort of environment you use.

These patterns are independent of the tools you use. Some tools support some of these concepts explicitly, some less directly. But the concepts have proved themselves useful in many development environments. For example, some tools don't support branching and merging as well as other tools. Clearly, you do not want to do these practices routinely without tool support, but at times even rudimentary support for branching will make your life easier than avoiding branching. Where appropriate, we discuss tool support in general terms so that you can see what features you need if you are looking for tools. We discuss examples using common tools, but we try to keep them at a level that will allow the book to stay current as tool interfaces change.

The pattern language in this book focuses on a team of developers working off of one codeline (or a small number of them) for any given release. These developers work in their own private workspaces.

Some issues of codeline organization for *large* projects we do not address in full, but the book is more about how things work in a local development environment. For a wide range of systems, the principles hold equally well.

## OVERVIEW OF THE LANGUAGE

Figure 3–1 shows the patterns in this language. The arrows show the relationships between the patterns that the context and unresolved issues section of each pattern describe. An arrow from one pattern (A) to another (B) means that pattern A is in the context of pattern B. This means pattern B is most useful once you have already thought about using pattern A. The arrow from A to B also means that pattern A needs pattern B to be complete.

The patterns in this pattern language can guide you toward establishing an active development environment that balances speed with thoroughness so that you can produce a good product quickly. After the first two patterns, the patterns fall into two groups: patterns that describe the structure of your workspace and patterns that describe the structure of your codelines.

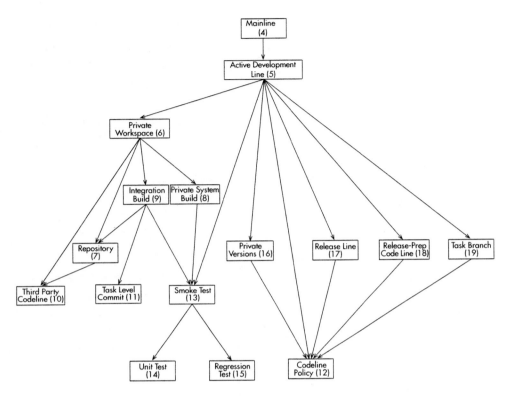

FIGURE 3–1.  The SCM pattern language

There are other approaches to development than the *Mainline* approach we discuss here. The *Mainline* approach works well in many circumstances, and other approaches may share many of the same patterns. It is important to remember as you read through these patterns that, although we hope this advice is useful, only you understand your set of circumstances. Apply the patterns with care.

The patterns in the language can be grouped into two sets: codeline-related patterns and workspace-related patterns.

The codeline-related patterns help you organize your source code and other artifacts appropriately, in terms of both structure and time

The patterns relating to codelines are[1]

---

1. References to patterns show the name of the pattern followed by the chapter number in parentheses.

- *Mainline (4)*

- *Active Development Line (5)*

- *Codeline Policy (12)*

- *Private Versions (16)*

- *Release Line (17)*

- *Release-Prep Code Line (18)*

- *Task Branch (19)*

Figure 3–2 shows these patterns.

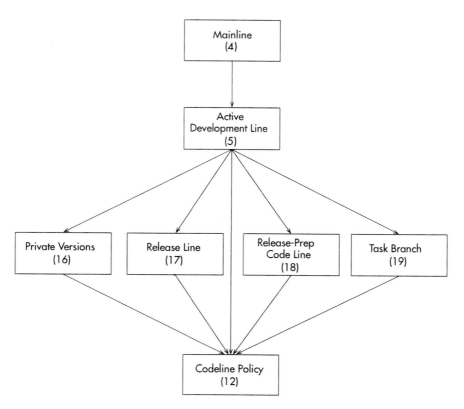

FIGURE 3–2. Codeline-related patterns

Figure 3–3 shows patterns related to workspaces.

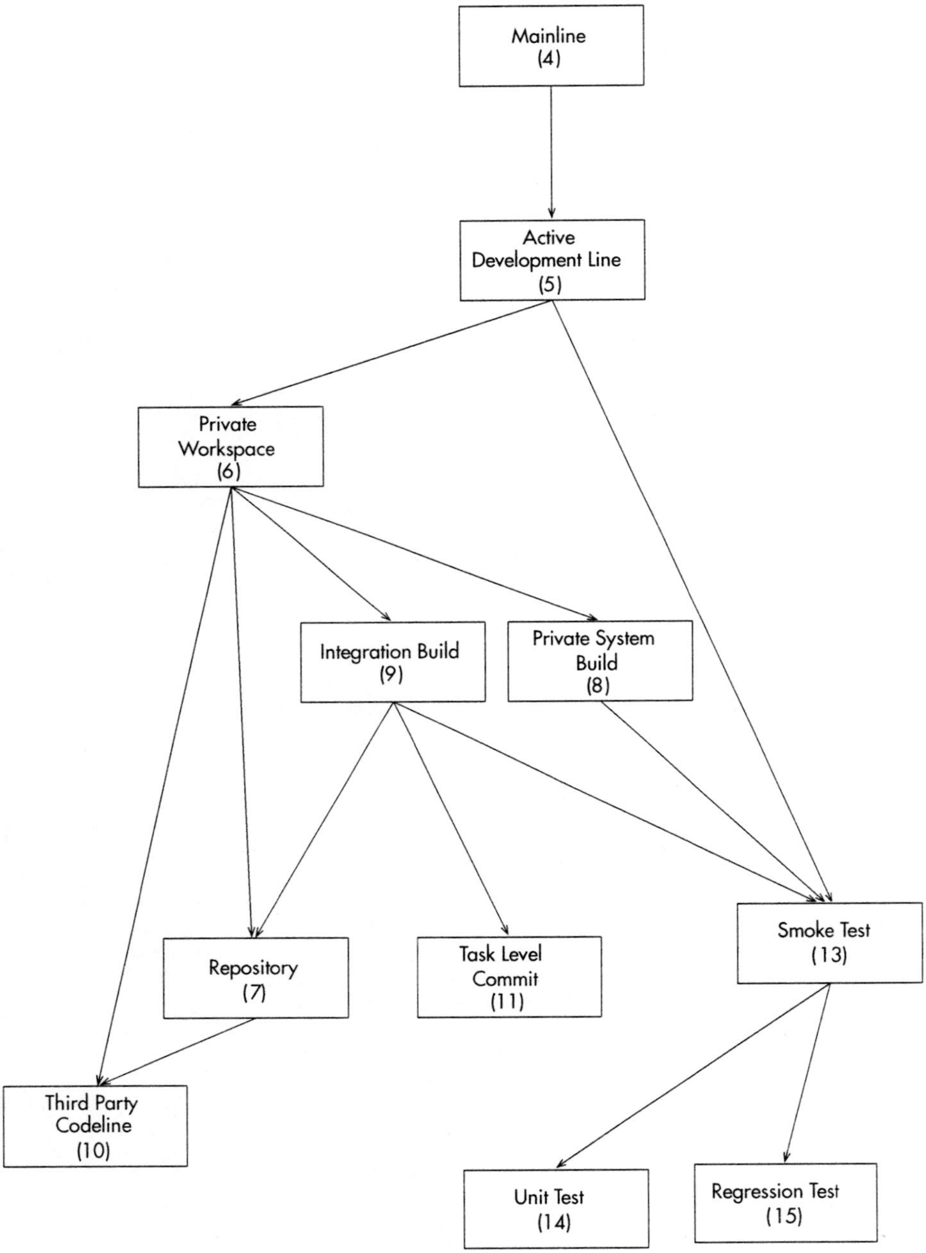

FIGURE 3–3. Workspace-related patterns

The patterns related to workspaces are

- *Private Workspace (6)*
- *Repository (7)*
- *Private System Build (8)*
- *Integration Build (9)*
- *Third Party Codeline (10)*
- *Task Level Commit (11)*
- *Smoke Test (13)*
- *Unit Test (14)*
- *Regression Test (15)*

## UNRESOLVED ISSUES

This chapter gives you an overview of pattern languages in general and the pattern language in this book. The rest of the book defines the patterns.

## FURTHER READING

- The series of books by Alexander et al. describes the core principles of patterns and pattern languages. *A Pattern Language* (Alexander et al. 1977) gives a pattern language for building towns and buildings. *The Timeless Way of Building* (Alexander 1979) describes the principles behind patterns and pattern languages. *The Oregon Experiment* (Alexander et al. 1975) gives a concrete example of using a pattern language in a real situation. Some of these books are a bit long, and Alexander's prose is a bit tough to wade through at times (with some examples of marginally correct grammar), but the ideas the book expresses are excellent.

- Many of the patterns for software systems were presented in workshops at the Pattern Languages of Programs conferences. A good collection of the patterns from these conferences appears in the *Pattern Languages of*

*Program Design* series (Coplien and Schmidt 1995; Vlissides et al. 1996; Martin et al. 1998; Harrison et al. 2000).

- The Hillside Group's patterns page is a good starting point for all things relating to software patterns, including information on the various patterns conferences. The URL is http://www.hillside.net/patterns.

- For examples of patterns applied to software systems, *Design Patterns* (Gamma et al. 1995) is the one book "everyone" has read. The *Pattern-Oriented Software Architecture* series of books is another example. These books do not approach the richness of the Alexander books, but they provide a concrete example.

- Brandon Goldfedder's *The Joy of Patterns* (Goldfedder 2002) is an excellent introduction to using the design patterns.

- *The Manager Pool: Patterns for Radical Leadership* (Olson and Stimmel 2002) is a collection of patterns on managing software organizations.

- *The Patterns Almanac* (Rising 2000) is one of the most comprehensive indexes of the state of software patterns in publication.

# Part II
## The Patterns

# 4

# Mainline

*On the main line.*
*Bowdle, South Dakota.*
*February 1942.*

*Photo by John Vachon. Library of Congress,*
*Prints & Photographs Division, FSA-OWI Collection,*
*Reproduction Number: LC-USF34-064602-D DLC.*

When you are developing a software application as part of a team effort, you often have to reconcile parallel development efforts. Your version control tool provides branching and merging facilities. You can use branches to isolate parallel efforts, but this can have a cost. This pattern shows you how to manage your codeline to minimize the integration effort that branching and merging require.

Y  *How do you keep the number of currently active codelines to a manageable set and avoid growing the project's version tree too wide and too dense? How do you minimize the overhead of merging?*

Generically, a branch is a means to organize file versions and show their history (White 2000). More specifically, a branch is a configuration of a system that is derived from, and developing independently of, the base configuration. For example, a branch can consist of a snapshot of the system at release time and all patches that you apply to the release. A branch can also be used to keep a subset of files that when merged with the main system, produce a unique variant, such as a platform-specific version or a customer variant.

Branching is a powerful mechanism for isolating yourself from change. You can branch to isolate changes for a release, for a platform, for a subsystem, for a developer's work—just about anytime you have work that goes off in a different direction. Whenever branches need to be integrated, you need to merge the changes—for example, when you must integrate a bug fix for the last release into the current release. This isolation from change can have a cost. Even with good tools, merging can be difficult because it is possible to make

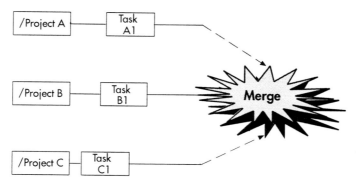

FIGURE 4–1. A merge can be messy.

two changes that conflict with each other (because of the intent of the change, if for no other reason), and you have no way of resolving the conflict without knowing the intention of the authors. You may have to make the change manually in both codelines. Any work you thought you would save by branching can be more than compensated for in the effort of a messy merge. Figure 4–1 illustrates this.

Separate codelines seem like a natural way to organize work in some cases. As your product evolves, you may want to create more codelines to isolate and organize changes. This is helpful because it is easy to allow the codelines to evolve in their own way. More codelines may mean more merging though, and more merging means more synchronization effort, and the practical costs of the merge may outweigh the apparent improved organization.

Some codelines are naturally derivative. It may be natural to think of each release using the prior release as a starting point, following a promotion model. This will give you a staircase codeline structure that can make it hard to determine where code originated, and making an urgent fix to a release without interrupting new development can be difficult with this structure. Figure 4–2 shows this case. But with this structure, the policy of the codeline will change from being active to development, and it requires developers to relocate work in progress to another codeline (Wingerd and Seiwald 1998).

Another use of a branch is to allow a subset of the team to work on a change with far-reaching consequences. If they work on the branch, they do not have to worry about breaking existing code or about problems other people's changes can cause. The branch isolates each group from changes

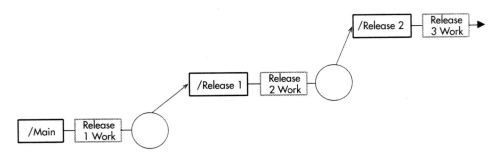

FIGURE 4–2.  Staircase branching (or a cascade)

another makes. This works well when you integrate back with the main body of code as quickly as possible, but if you branch simply to defer integration, the merge will be difficult, and you are just putting off the inevitable.

Some argue for resisting the temptation to ever delay integration. Extreme Programming advocates continuous integration because the effort of integration is exponentially proportional to the amount of time between integrations (Fowler and Foemmel 2002), but sometimes parts of the code base really are evolving in different directions, and independent lines of evolution make sense.

## FEAR OF BRANCHING

People seem to be both fascinated by and fearful of branching. This ambiguity is often caused by people not understanding their tools and not understanding their motivations for branching.

Branching (like most everything else) when done without good, sound reasoning can hinder more than help. It is admittedly very easy to go branch-happy or branch-crazy and use it too much. Branching should be done in moderation and with careful consideration. Going to great lengths to avoid it, however, can often cause you more work in the end. So just as one should not branch "on whim," take care not to go to the other extreme of taking a lot of measures to avoid it, based more on fear and the lack of information. *continued*

A great deal can also depend on the version control tool you use. Branching in a tool such as VSS is very limited in capability, somewhat unwieldy, and not often recommended. Branching in CVS is much easier but still not as nice as with tools that have much better logical and visual support for branching or built-in intelligence to know which "paths" have already been merged.

I have worked at places where someone discovers the branching facilities of a tool and then starts using them without thinking out a strategy. The branches create isolation, but they sometimes isolate too much. The product reaches a point where they have a "staircase" branching structure: Each branch has other branches off of it, and each of these branches is fairly long-lived and active. Then when the time comes for a major change that affects many of the "branches," the only good way to integrate the change is to add it manually to all the branches. When people discuss situations like this with me, they quickly talk about how bad their tool is because it won't support their structure. They rarely discuss whether the structure actually made sense.

The reality often is that the structure does not fit the business model of the company. A simpler branching model would have worked better in practice. Also, the extent to which the company is willing to invest in tool support to allow complicated merges also indicates how complicated a branching structure they need. I've found that if you can't make a case for a tool that supports a complicated branch-and-merge structure, management doesn't understand why there should be such a structure.

At the other end of the spectrum are the people who decide never to branch. Often they had been in a situation where the branching and merging was hellish, and they avoid branches at all costs. This is, of course, shortsighted because there are many valid reasons to branch a codeline. As with any tool, you should understand how to use it and how it can hurt you if you use it badly.

If you want to branch, creating a branch can be a simple matter with the right tools, but a branch is a fairly heavyweight thing. A branch of a project can be all the components for a release and some of their dependents. So creating that branch has serious consequences if you need to integrate any changes from the original codeline into it.

If you don't branch, you lose the isolation a branch gives you, and your code all needs to work together for anyone to get anything done. But in most cases, your code needs to work together in the end anyway. You need to balance the transient freedom that branching gives you with the costs that you will encounter when you need to resynchronize.

You want to maximize the concurrency on your codelines while minimizing problems that deferred integration can cause.

## SIMPLIFY YOUR BRANCHING MODEL

> Y *When you are developing a single product release, develop off of a mainline. A mainline is a "home codeline" that you do all your development on except in special circumstances. When you do branch, consider your overall strategy before you create the branch. When in doubt, go for a simpler model.*

The reason for a mainline is to have "a central codeline to act as a basis for subbranches and their resultant merges" (Vance 1998). The mainline for a project generally starts with the code base for the previous release or version. If you are doing new development, you start with only one codeline, which is your mainline by definition.

Doing mainline development does not mean "do not branch." It means that all ongoing development activities end up on a single codeline at some time.

Don't start a branch unless you have a clear reason for it and the effort of a later merge is greatly outweighed by the independence of the branch. Favor branches that won't have to be merged often—for example, release lines. Branching can be a powerful tool, but like any tool, it should be treated with respect and understanding. Do most of your development work off of a mainline. Use good build and development practices to ensure that what is checked in to the mainline is usable, but realize that the tip of the mainline is a work in progress and will not always be of release quality.

Do most of your work on one codeline. The mainline need not be the root of the version control system. It can be a branch that you are starting a new effort on. The key idea is that all the work done on a release will be integrated quickly into one codeline.

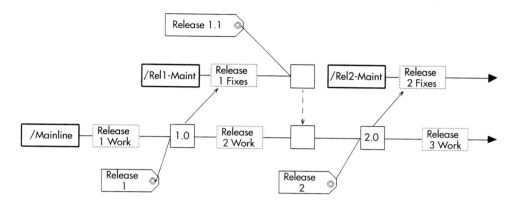

FIGURE 4–3. Mainline development

You need to ensure that the code in the mainline always works reasonably. It is to your advantage to maintain a continually integrated system anyway because "big-bang" integration costs almost always exceed expectations.

When the time comes to create a codeline for a new major release, instead of branching the new release line from the previous release line, merge the previous release line back to the mainline branch and branch the new release line from there. Have a shallow branching model, such as shown in Figure 4–3.

Mainline development offers the following advantages.

- Having a mainline reduces merging and synchronization effort by requiring fewer transitive change propagations.

- A mainline provides closure by bringing changes back to the overall workstream instead of leaving them splintered and fragmented.

There are still reasons to branch. You should branch toward the end of a release cycle to isolate a stable version of the code base at that revision level. This will enable you to fix bugs on that branch without introducing new features and other work in progress to the already released codeline.

Limit branching to special situations, including the following.

- Customer releases. This allows bug-fix development on the release code without exposing the customer to new feature work in progress on the mainline. You may want to migrate bug fixes between the release branches and the mainline, but depending on the nature of the work on each line, this too may be limited.

- Long-lived parallel efforts that multiple people will be working on. If this work will make the codeline more unstable than usual, create a *Task Branch (19)*. This works best when the mainline will have only small changes done on it.

- Integration. When you create customer release lines, instead of doing a code freeze, create an integration branch on which your developers will do all their work. This allows progress to continue on the mainline. Bug fixes in the integration line need to be integrated into the mainline, but this should not be too difficult because the release should be close to what is currently active.

Some situations will still require a branch. But generally you should think hard before branching; ask yourself if the work really requires a branch. Branches have many uses, but you want to avoid long-lived branches that must be merged later.

To do mainline development:

- Create a codeline (e.g. /main) using the current active code base as a starting point.

- Check in all changes to this codeline.

- Follow appropriate precheck-in test procedures to keep this mainline useful and correct.

Mainline development can greatly simplify your development process. Wingerd and Seiwald report that "90% of SCM 'process' is enforcing codeline promotion to compensate for the lack of a mainline" (Wingerd and Seiwald 1998).

## UNRESOLVED ISSUES

Once you decide to have a mainline, you need to figure out how to keep the mainline usable when many people are working on it. *Active Development Line (5)* describes how to manage this.

## FURTHER READING

- SCM tool manuals, such as those for CVS and ClearCase, describe how to manage mainline and release line development. You can download and find out about CVS at http://www.cvshome.com/.

- *Open Source Development with CVS* (Fogel and Bar 2001) describes how to use the popular open source tool CVS.

- *Software Release Methodology,* by Michael Bays (Bays 1999), has a good discussion about branching strategies and issues for merging.

- *Software Configuration Management Strategies and Rational ClearCase* (White 2000) discusses branching strategies. Although the book focuses on ClearCase, there is also good generic information in the book.

# 5

# Active Development Line

*Construction, Grand Central Terminal, New York, between 1905 and 1915.*

You have an evolving codeline that has code intended to work with a future product release. You are doing most of your work on a *Mainline (4)*. When you are working in a dynamic development environment, many people are changing the code. Team members are working toward making the system better, but any change can break the system, and changes can conflict. This pattern helps you balance stability and progress in an active development effort.

Y *How do you keep a rapidly evolving codeline stable enough to be useful?*

You develop software in teams because you want there to be concurrent work. The more people you have working on a code base, the more you need communication among team members. You also have more potential for conflicting changes.

For the team as a whole to make progress, you need synchronization points where the work comes together. As in any concurrent system, having a synchronization point means that we might have deadlock or blocking if we don't manage the coordination correctly. Deadlock can happen when two people have mutual dependencies, and a check-in before a test finishes could mean that the test would fail the next time we ran it. Blocking can happen when the precheck-in process takes too long and someone else needs the changes to proceed.

If we think of software development as a set of concurrent processes, we have to synchronize whenever we check in a change to the codeline in the source control system. When someone checks in a change to the codeline, that person can cause delays for the whole team if the change breaks someone else's work. Even if we tested the change with what we thought was the latest code, it could still be incompatible with the change that was checked in moments before. But if we put too much effort into testing for changes, making sure that a change works with every change that was checked in while we were running the last set of tests, we may not be able to check in our changes in a reasonable amount of time. That can cause delays too.

Working from a highly tested stable line isn't always an option when you are developing new features. You want to use your version control system to exchange work in progress for integration, and there may be many features that you don't have integration tests for yet because they are so new.

You want to be able to get current code from the source control system and have a reasonable expectation that it will work. You want the codeline to be stable so that it does not interfere with people's work. You can require that people perform simple procedures before submitting code to the codeline, such as a preliminary build and some level of testing. These tests take time, though, and the delay between check-ins may work against some of the project's greater goals. A broken codeline slows down everyone who works from it, but the time it takes to test exhaustively slows down people as well, and in some cases can provide a false sense of security because you can never fully test a system that is in flux. Even if you do test your code before check-in, concurrency issues mean that two changes, tested individually, will result in the second one breaking the system. And the more exhaustive—and longer running—your tests are, the more likely it is that a noncompatible change may be submitted, as Figure 5–1 shows.

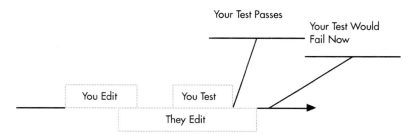

FIGURE 5–1. Long-running tests have mixed value

## TESTING TREADMILL

I have worked at a number of start-up companies, and there is a recurring theme that goes like this. Initially, only a few people are working on the product. They understand what they are doing very well, and even when they step on each other's work, they recover quickly. Then the company grows, and the code in version control is hardly ever consistent. The tip of the mainline always breaks. In frustration, someone sets up test suites that people should run before doing a check-in to the source control system. The first cut at this test suite is every test they can think of. The test suite grows, and soon it takes an hour to run the precheck-in tests. People compensate by checking in code less often, causing pain when there are merges or other integration issues. Productivity goes down as well. Someone suggests shortening the test suites, but they are met with resistance justified by cries of "We are doing this to ensure quality." Someone else comments that "the pain is worth it, considering what we went through last year when we had no tests."

But, once we reached a basic level of stability, the emphasis on exhaustive testing led to diminishing returns as progress as a whole was reduced. This gets worse when the tests are not exhaustive but simply exhausting to the developers who run them.

You can prevent changes from being checked in to the codeline while you are testing by using semaphores, but then only one person at a time can test and check in changes, which can also slow progress. Figure 5–2 shows a very stable but very slowly evolving codeline.

You can also make changes to your codeline structure to keep parts of the code tree stable, creating branches at various points, but that adds complexity and requires a merge.

FIGURE 5–2. A stable but dead codeline

FIGURE 5–3. A very active but very useless codeline

You can go to the other extreme and make your codeline a free-for-all. Figure 5–3 shows a quickly evolving but unusable codeline.

You can also change the module architecture of the system to reduce the likelihood of conflicting change, but even then you may still have two people changing the code in a way that breaks something.

Aiming for perfection is likely to fail in all but the most static environments. You can achieve stability on a given codeline but with process and synchronization overhead, increased merging, and more complicated maintenance and administration. This is not always worthwhile. You want a balance: an active codeline that will, more likely than not, be usable most of the time.

## DEFINE YOUR GOALS

Y *Institute policies that are effective in making your main development line stable enough for the work it needs to do. Do not aim for a perfect active development line but for a mainline that is usable and active enough for your needs.*

An active development line will have frequent changes, some well-tested checkpoints that are guaranteed to be "good," and other points in the codeline that are likely to be good enough for someone to do development on the tip of the line. Figure 5–4 shows what this looks like.

The hard part of this solution is figuring out how "good" your codeline needs to be. You need to go through a process similar to doing a

FIGURE 5–4. An active, alive codeline

requirements analysis for building a software system. Your clients want perfection and completeness, and they want it quickly and cheaply. These goals are, in reality, unattainable. Do an analysis along the following lines.

- Who uses the codeline?

- What is the release cycle?

- What test mechanisms do we have in place?

- How much is the system evolving?

- What are the real costs for a cycle where things are broken?

For example, if the codeline is being used by other teams that are also doing active development, some instability is appropriate, and the emphasis should be on speed. If this is the beginning of the new development or if the team is adding many new features, you expect more instability. If this codeline is basically stable and being used as a standard component, more validation is appropriate. Right before you want to branch or freeze for a release, you want more stability, so you want to test more.

Understand your project's rhythm. Dikel and Kane define rhythm as "the recurring, predictable exchange of work products within an architecture group and across customers and suppliers"(Dikel et al. 2001). A good project rhythm is especially important for architecture-centric development, but any project that has concurrent work with dependencies needs a good rhythm. The source control structure can influence how the rhythm is executed, and culture helps define what rhythm you need.

If you have good unit and regression tests, run either by developers or as part of the system build postcheck-in, errors will not persist as long, so emphasize speed on check-in. If you do not have a good testing infrastructure, be more careful until you develop it. If you want to add functionality, emphasize speed.

If clients need a good deal of stability, they should use only *Named Stable Bases (20)* of the components, enabling them to avoid "cutting edge" work in progress. Figure 5–5 shows how these baselines are identified and labeled

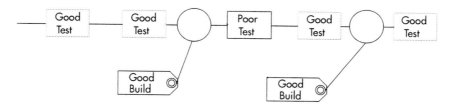

FIGURE 5–5. Labeling Named Stable Bases

when they pass tests. But these clients should then be treated more like external clients than members of the active development team.

Don't be too conservative. People can work with any system as long as they understand the trade-offs and the needs. You don't want to make the check-in process too difficult. If you have a precheck-in process that takes a long time, you run the risk of developers doing larger-grained and less frequent check-ins, which will slow feature progress. Less frequent check-ins increase the possibility of a conflict during testing and make it harder to back out a problematic change.

Establish criteria for how much to test the code before check-ins.

The standard needs to set a quality level that is strict enough to keep showstopper defects out of the daily build, but lenient enough to disregard trivial defects (because undue attention to trivial defects can paralyze progress) (McConnell 1996).

Martin Fowler suggests for the purposes of continuous integration (Fowler and Foemmel 2002) that a selected suite of tests run against the system successfully. The more exhaustive the tests, the longer the precheck-in time. You need to determine how much stability is *really* necessary for your purposes.

Remember that there is a fundamental difference between code that is close to release and code that is being actively changed. If you need a stable codeline, perhaps what you want isn't the active development line but a fully tested and verified *Release Line (17)*. There are significant benefits in the form of catching potential problems early in developing with an *Active Development Line (5)*. You can also push off your more exhaustive testing to a batch process that creates your *Named Stable Bases (20)*.

To prevent total chaos on the mainline, set up each developer with a *Private Workspace (6)* where each can do a *Private System Build (8)*, *Unit Test (14)*, and *Smoke Test (13)*.

Have an integration workspace where snapshots of the code are built periodically and subjected to more exhaustive tests.

Any SCM tool that supports "triggers," or automatic events that happen after a change is submitted, will help automate the process of verifying that you are meeting the quality metric. You can then set up the system to run a build or a set of tests after a change is submitted. You can also set up the system to run less often.

As Jim Highsmith writes, "Change is expensive, no question about it. However, consider the alternative—stagnation" (Highsmith 2002).

## UNRESOLVED ISSUES

Once you have established that a "good enough" codeline is desirable, you need to identify the codeline that will be like this. *Codeline Policy (12)* will establish which lines follow this form and what the check-in/commit process is for these (and other) codelines.

Individual developers still need isolation to keep the *Active Development Line (5)* alive. They can do this by working in a *Private Workspace (6)*.

When the need for stability approaches, some work will need to be broken off to a *Release-Prep Code Line (18)*.

Some long-lived tasks may need more stability than an active development line can provide, even though you realize that there may be an integration cost later. For these, use a *Task Branch (19)*. Doing this also insulates the primary codeline from high-risk changes.

## FURTHER READING

- One reason people resist applying this pattern is that they think their problem is that code is not perfect, when in fact the problem is that it is too hard to change and evolve the code. A great book about getting to the core of the "real" problem is *Are Your Lights On?* (Gause and Weinberg 1990).

- *Agile Software Development Ecosystems* (Highsmith 2002) discusses the reality of continuous change in most projects.

# 6

# Private Workspace

*A government clerk's room, showing a desk with books, telephone and directory, and a desk lamp on it. Washington, D.C., 1939.*

*Photo by David Meyers. Library of Congress, Prints & Photographs Division, FSA-OWI Collection, Reproduction Number: LC-USF33-015598-M2.*

In *Active Development Line (5)*, you and other developers make frequent changes to the code base, both to the modules you are working on and to modules you depend on. You want to be sure you are working with the latest code, but because people don't deal well with uncontrolled change, you want to be in control when you start working with other developers' changes. This pattern describes how you can reconcile the tension between always developing with a current code base and the reality that people cannot work effectively when their environment is in constant flux.

Y *How do you do keep current with a continuously changing codeline and also make progress without being distracted by your environment changing out from under you?*

Developers need a place where they can work on their code, isolated from outside changes, while they are finishing a task.

When a team develops software, people work in parallel, with the hope that the team gets work done more quickly than any individual. Each individual makes changes in parallel with the other team members. You now have the problem of managing and integrating these parallel streams of change. Writing and debugging code, on the other hand, is a fairly linear activity. Because in team development, concurrent changes are happening to the codeline while you are working on your specific changes, there is a tension between keeping up to date with the current state of the codeline and the human tendency to work best in an environment of minimal change. Changes that distract you from your primary purpose interrupt your flow.

DeMarco and Lister define "flow" as "a condition of deep, nearly meditative involvement"(DeMarco and Lister 1987). In *Peopleware*, the authors discuss flow as noise and task-related interruptions, but integrating a change that is not related to the task at hand can have a similar effect.

Developing software in a team environment involves the following steps:

- Writing and testing your code changes

- Integrating your code with the work that other people were doing

There are two extreme approaches to managing parallel change: literal continuous integration and delayed integration.

You can integrate every change team members make as soon as they make it. This is the clearest way to know whether your changes work with the current state of the codeline. The downside of this "continuous integration" into your workspace approach is that you may spend much of your time integrating, handling changes tangential to your task. Frequent integration helps you isolate when a flaw appeared. Integrating too many changes at once can make it harder to isolate where the flaw is because it can be in one of the many changes that have happened since you integrated. Figure 6–1 shows this concept.

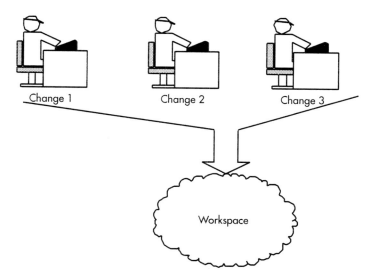

FIGURE 6–1. Combining changes at once

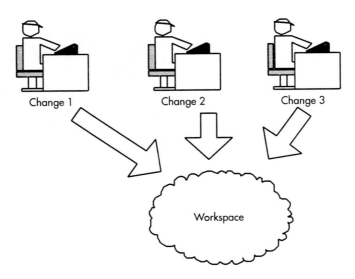

Change 1            Change 2            Change 3

Workspace

Figure 6–2. Integrating each change as it happens

Even when you do "continuous integration," as when you are doing
Extreme Programming, you really integrate in discrete steps, as when a day's
work is complete. Figure 6–2 shows this case.

You can integrate at the last possible moment. This makes it simplest for
you, the developer, while you are working, but it means that you may have
many outside integration issues to deal with, meaning that it will take longer
to integrate at the end.

You can "help" developers keep up to date by having them work from a
shared source/release area, keeping only local copies of the components
they are modifying. Figure 6–3 illustrates this. But you don't want things
to change unexpectedly. Also, a change in one of the other components
can affect your work. If you are coding in a language such as C++, a
change in a header can cause a compilation problem. A change in the
source can cause a behavior problem. Even with a highly modular architecture, components interact, making it hard to get consistent results
across a change.

Sometimes you are working on things other than the latest code base. You
must interrupt your work on the current release to work on the code at an

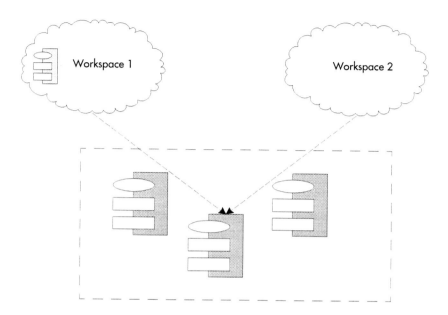

FIGURE 6–3.  Sharing some components between workspaces

## A SIMPLE PLAN

To some, this sounds like an easy-to-solve problem with an obvious solution. When I was interviewing for a job at a start-up company six years into my career, I discovered that some obvious solutions are easy to miss if you are not thinking about the context. The company had fully bought into the idea of nightly builds. The problem was that each developer worked from a shared product area, so after a night of working on a problem, you could come in the next day to find that your development environment had changed dramatically and then have to spend half the day simply getting to where you were the night before.

This illustrates one problem with blindly following a "good idea" without thinking through the reasons for using it.

earlier point in time. Or you may need to experiment with a new feature. Sometimes you can't be up to date and still do your work.

You can also avoid the problems of continuous updates by taking a snapshot of the entire system and performing all your coding tasks against the snapshot. This overly conservative approach can cause problems when you get behind the leading edge of changes. You may find yourself introducing problems into the global environment.

You need a way to control the rate of change in the code you are developing without falling too far out of step with the evolving codeline.

## ISOLATE YOUR WORK TO CONTROL CHANGE

> Y   *Do your work in a private workspace, where you control the versions of code and components you are working on. You will have total control over when and how your environment changes.*

Every team member should be able to set up a workspace where there is a consistent version of the software. A concise definition of a workspace is "a copy of all the 'right' versions of all the 'right' files in the 'right' directories" (White 2000). A workspace is also a place "where an item evolves through many temporary and inconsistent states until is checked into the library" (Whitgift 1991). You should have total control of when parts of the system change. You control when changes are integrated into your workspace. The most common situation is when you are working on the tip of the codeline along with other team members, but when you are working on a version that is not the latest, you can re-create any configuration necessary.

A *private workspace* comprises the following.

- Source code you are editing.

- Any locally built components.

- Third-party derived objects that you cannot or do not wish to build.

- Built objects for all the code in the system. You can build these yourself, have references to a shared repository (with the correct version), or have copies of built objects.

- Configuration and data that you need to run and test the system.
- Build scripts to build the system in your workspace.
- Information identifying the versions of all the components in the system.

A *private workspace* should not contain the following.

- Private versions of systemwide scripts that enforce policy. These should be in a shared binary directory so that all users get the latest functionality.
- Components that are in version control but that you copied from somewhere else. You should be able to reproduce the state of your workspace consistently when you are performing a task, by referencing a version identifier for every component in the workspace.
- Any tools (compilers, and so on) that must be the same across all versions of the product. If different versions of the product require different versions of tools, the build scripts can address this by selecting the appropriate tool versions for a configuration.

In addition, a *private workspace* can include tools that facilitate your work, as long as the tools are compatible with the work style of the team.

To do your coding for mainline development, follow a procedure similar to this.

1. Get up to date. Update the source tree from the codeline you are working on so that you are working with the current code and build, or repopulate the workspace from the latest system build. If you are working on a different branch or label, create a new *private workspace* from that branch.

2. Make your changes. Edit the components you need to change.

3. Do a *Private System Build (8)* to update any derived objects.

4. Test your change with a *Unit Test (14)*.

5. Update the workspace to the latest versions of all other components by getting the latest versions of all components you have not changed.

6. Rebuild. Run a *Smoke Test (13)* to make sure that you have not broken anything.

If your system is small enough, you can simply get the source and any binary objects for the correct configuration of all the product components and build the entire system. You might also consider getting the latest code from the *Mainline (4)* and building the entire system if it does not take too long. This will ensure that the system you are running matches the source code. With a good incremental build environment, doing this should work rather well, allowing for, perhaps, the one-time cost of the whole system build.

In more complex systems or where you are especially intolerant of problems, populate the environment by getting the source and object files from a known good build (*Named Stable Bases (20)*). You can also get all the source files from the *Mainline (4)* because this will probably simplify debugging. Get whatever external components you need from the *Third Party Codeline (10)*. All these components should be of the correct configuration (version, label, and so on) for the system you are working on. Get private versions of all the source components you will be changing.

If you are working on multiple tasks, you can have multiple workspaces, each with its own configuration. For example, you can have a release 1.1 workspace to fix problems in the old release while doing new development in a release 2 workspace. These can be separate and complete workspaces. It is not worth the effort, in most cases, to save space by factoring out common components. (For example, if component X has not changed between release 1.1 and release 2, it is worthwhile simply to have two copies of this component. If X changes in release 2 later on, it will be easy to update the release 2 workspace without affecting the release 1 workspace.

Be sure that any tests, scripts, tools, and so on use the correct execution paths so that they run with the correct workspace version and not with a component from another workspace or an installed version of the product. One way to do this is to deploy all local components in one binary directory and put the current directory in the path. Another way is to start tests in a script that sets the environment.

Some component environments, such as COM, define certain items machinewide, so be sure to have a mechanism to switch between workspaces by unregistering and registering the appropriate servers.

To be sure that you have built all dependencies, do a *Private System Build (8)*. Check that your changes integrate successfully with the work others have done in the meantime by getting the latest code from the *Mainline (4)* (exclusive of changes you have made). If you are working on multiple tasks at one time, your workspace should have many workspaces.

One risk with a *Private Workspace (6)* is that developers will work with old "known" code too long, and they will be working with outdated code. You can protect yourself from this by doing a periodic *Private System Build (8)* and making sure that changes do not break the build or fail the *Smoke Test (13)*. (The sidebar Update Your Workspace to Keep Current discusses the *workspace update* in more detail.)

The easiest way to avoid becoming out of date is to do fine-grained tasks, checking in your changes after each one and updating your workspace before starting a new task. Some people find it useful to establish a discipline of creating a brand-new workspace periodically to avoid problems that stray files might cause and preventing the "works for me" syndrome. This is not ideal but is an adaptation to the reality that some version control tools do an imperfect job of updating, particularly when you move files within the system.

Having a *Private Workspace (6)* does take more space than working with shared source, but the simplicity it adds to your work is worth it.

An automated build process should also have its own workspace. Set up the workspace to always get all the updates, if you are doing a "latest" build.

Good tool support makes managing a combination of shared and private components easy, but you can get quite far by using basic version control tools and scripts. For example, if your system can be built quickly but uses some third-party components, your checkout process can populate your workspace from version control with all the source from your system and the built objects for the third-party components. After you build your product code, you will have a complete system.

A *Smoke Test (13)* allows you to check that your changes don't break the functionality of the system in a major way. A well-designed smoke test will help you minimize the amount of code you need to keep in your workspace and rebuild, because the Smoke Tests should test the features that clients of your module expect.

Some work touches large parts of the code base and takes a long time to finish. In these cases, a *Task Branch (19)* may be the more appropriate approach.

Depending on your specific goal, there are a number of variations to this pattern, including a developer workspace, an integration workspace, and a task workspace, in which case a developer has a number of workspaces in the area concurrently.

Variations of a workspace are used for specific purposes—for example, an integration workspace, which is where changes are combined with the current state of the system, built, and tested. This can also be called a build workspace and may exist on the integration or build machine.

## UPDATE YOUR WORKSPACE TO KEEP CURRENT

After a workspace has been populated, the codeline may continue to evolve. If the work in your workspace is isolated for too long, the versions in the workspace can become outdated. A *workspace update* operation will "refresh" the outdated versions in your workspace, replacing them with the versions from the latest stable state of the codeline. If any of the files you changed are also among the set of "newer" files from the codeline, merge conflicts may occur and will need to be reconciled.

You should do a workspace update before you merge your changes back to the codeline during a *Task Level Commit (11)*. You will need to rebuild using a *Private System Build (8)*, or at least recompile immediately after the update, to find and fix quickly any inconsistencies introduced by the new changes. If desired, immediately before updating your workspace, checkpoint it using a label or *Private Versions (16)* to ensure that you can roll back to its previous state.

You may also update your workspace at known stable points, as well as right before you are about to check out a new set of files, to ensure that your workspace remains stable without growing "stale." This enables you to find out early on if any recently committed changes conflict with any changes in your workspace. You may then reconcile those changes in your *Private Workspace (6)* at incremental intervals, instead of waiting until the end to do all of them at once.

## UNRESOLVED ISSUES

Once you have stability for yourself, you still need to prevent introducing errors into the system when you check in your changes. *Private System Build (8)* lets you check that your system does not break the build and also enables you to do an incremental build for the parts of your system when you do an incremental update from version control for other components.

You need to populate your workspace from a *Repository (7)* containing all the source and related components. Externally provided components need to come from a *Third Party Codeline (10)*.

Once you are done with your local work, it must be incorporated into the rest of the system in an *Integration Build (9)*.

## FURTHER READING

- Brian White in *Software Configuration Management Strategies and Rational ClearCase: A Practical Introduction* (White 2000) has a good description of the various types of workspaces that ClearCase supports (ClearCase calls them "views"). He says that "one of the essential functions of an SCM tool is to establish and manage the developers' working environment, often referred to as a 'workspace' or a 'sandbox.'"

- Private workspaces are a common practice in successful development organizations, so common that they are often not described as such. Managing change, consistent build practices, and other essential components of private workspaces are all part of the practices that classic books such as *Code Complete* (McConnell 1993) and *Rapid Development* (McConnell 1996), among others, describe.

7

# Repository

*Cases of canned salmon in warehouse. Astoria, Oregon, September 1941.*

*Photo by Russell Lee. Library of Congress, Prints & Photographs Division, FSA-OWI Collection, Reproduction Number: LC-USF33-013141-M1.*

79

To create a *Private Workspace (6)* or to run a reliable *Integration Build (9)*, you need the right components. This pattern shows you how to build a workspace easily from the necessary parts.

≈ *How do you get the right versions of the right components into a new workspace?*

Any software development activity you perform starts with a workspace where you have the components necessary to build, run, and test your software. You need the right versions of everything that makes up the system so that you can accurately diagnose problems before you check in changes.

You want to get the elements of your workspace easily so that you can reliably create an environment that allows you to do your work using the right versions of the software, whether you are working with the current active codeline or with an earlier version of the code base.

As Figure 7–1 shows, a workspace consists of more than just code. Some of the things you need include

- The source code you are working with

- Components you are not working with, as either source or library files

- Third-party components, such as jar files, libraries, DLLs, and so on, depending on your language and platform

- Configuration files

- Data files to initialize your application

- Build scripts and build environment settings so that you can get a consistent build

- Installation scripts for some components

Some of these elements have natural origins. You could get source code from your version control system, copy installation scripts for some components, and get third-party-built components from a development server. You can get other things that are not in source control from a server. Multiple locations for various resources add a lot of overhead to tasks for already busy software developers. You spend most of your coding time using tools such as an IDE, a compiler, and your version control system, and copying files from multiple source points leaves opportunity for error.

If you get tired of performing many manual operations to update your workspace, you may decide to write your own tool to keep your self in sync,

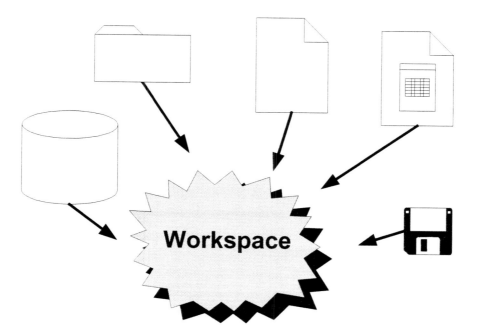

FIGURE 7–1. A workspace is created from many things

and you may even share the tool with the rest of the team. Although developing such tools will save you time, you still run the risk of having the tool get out of sync with any new locations or policies, and you may incur a maintenance burden for the tool that distracts you from your work.

You need to be sure to associate the right versions of each element. For example, you might switch versions of a third-party library in the middle of a product release cycle. You can keep people up to date about changes by communicating. You can tell them to use a new version of the database API classes, and they may remember to update at the right time. It is difficult, however, for people to keep track of these details reliably on their own. People could be in the middle of a task when they receive an e-mail about a change to a third-party component and forget to update their workspace after a task. It is difficult to remember what configurations went together for an earlier release.

A manual update process takes time. And if you missed the update notice, you may have a number of locations to check. This can take a lot of time, especially if the components are in different places.

Another issue is going back to the correct configuration at a certain point in time. You can maintain a list of configuration components and have people refer to it when re-creating a test environment, but that is prone to error.

You keep your source code in a version control system, and adding more places for people to look for things adds to the complexity of creating a new workspace. If it is too hard to create a workspace, you may feel a natural reluctance to keep up to date or to create another workspace to work on another codeline.

## ONE STOP SHOPPING

> *Have a single point of access, or a repository, for your code and related artifacts. Make creating a developer workspace as simple and transparent as possible.*

Make the mechanism you use to create a workspace simple and repeatable. You should be able to create a workspace that contains artifacts from any identifiable revision of the product, including third-party components and

## SO MANY TO CHOOSE FROM

Many times I have wanted to test our product while working from the tip of the active codeline rather than from the latest install. The latest install often lagged behind the codeline by a day or so, and I wanted to see whether a recent change that someone else made addressed a problem that I was having.

Because of the nature of the product and the structure of our organization, the development environment had only a portion of the configuration data and libraries from other groups up to date. There were nightly builds of these components, but they were staged into the development area when someone needed an update. So we could go for days or weeks without realizing that something had changed.

When I tried to test, there were many mismatches between the server and client components. After three days, I discovered the problem and wrote some scripts (with the help of our release team) to enable developers to get the latest library files and configuration files from the source control tree.

How did this situation arise? In part because of lack of communication between the release engineering team and the various product teams. And in part because of a desire to control change too much. It is admirable not to accept changes in an unexpected manner, but if a library component changed months ago, it is already in the product. If the development team cannot see a problem, they are wasting the company's time when they leave it to the QA team to find all the integration issues.

The problems start when developers can't reproduce bugs in their development environment because they are (unknowingly) out of sync with the released version. Or they are reluctant to work on the correct version of the code base because it takes too long to set up.

These places are in better shape than if they had no version control system, but they waste lots of developer time and energy.

built artifacts such as library files. The mechanism should also make it easy to determine whether there is a new version of an existing element or a new component that you need when you are working on the tip of a development. Figure 7–2 shows this.

There are many ways to implement this pattern, and the details depend on the features of your version control tool, your build environment, and, to a certain extent, your team's culture. There are three requirements for your implementation.

- It should be easy to use and repeatable. This is in the spirit of what Andy Hunt and Dave Thomas refer to as "Ubiquitous Automation" (Hunt and Thomas 2002a); (Hunt and Thomas 2002b).

- It should give you *all* the components you need to create a *Private Workspace (6)* for working on a particular state of your project, including build scripts and built objects.

- It should work for all versions of the project.

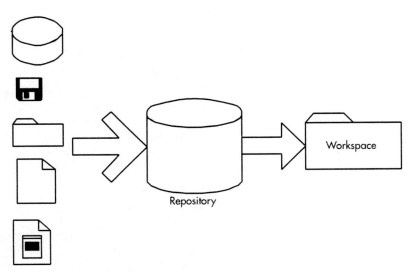

FIGURE 7–2. Populate your workspace from a repository

Some common implementations are using the version control system as a repository for all artifacts and using scripts in combination with the version control system.

Since you have a version control system, a straightforward way of implementing this pattern is to place all source files, configuration files, build scripts, and third-party components in it. Identify the set that is relevant to a particular version of product by using labels or creating a branch with the source codeline, third-party codeline, and so on. This makes it easy to create a new workspace. You issue the "get" command and specify the version of the product you want. You can now also identify when something changes. If a third-party component changes, your version control system's "update" command will get you a new version. If a component is the same as you already have, it will not update it (see Figure 7–3).

This way, the version control system mirrors the build environment, and the history of changes in the build environment can also be tracked.

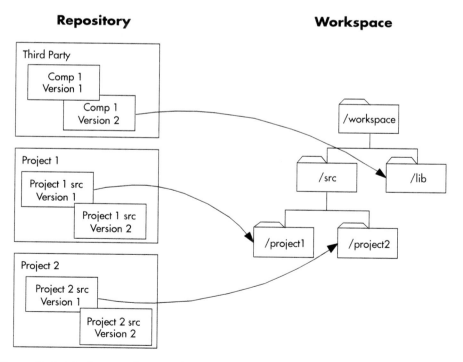

FIGURE 7–3. Version tree for a workspace

If (a) the version control tree is not a direct mapping to the build tree and your version control tool does not provide an easy way to perform the mapping, or (b) there is some reason not to keep every component in version control (some version control systems do not handle binary files well, and you may need to keep library files elsewhere if they do not change frequently), use a script or a makefile that copies the appropriate versions of the appropriate files to the appropriate places, depending on the version you want. This might be the easiest and best way to populate your workspace with the result of a nightly build.

All your configuration files and so on can also be tied together. If a new database library needs new configuration settings, you can give them the same label or check them in to the tip of the version tree together.

Some tools you can use to help you create this script are "make" and ANT. Both have interfaces to common version control systems.

## UNRESOLVED ISSUES

Organize third-party code using *Third Party Codeline (10).*

## FURTHER READING

- Tools such as "make" (http://www.gnu.org/software/make/make.html) and ANT (http://jakarta.apache.org/ant/) are very helpful in automating the process of keeping a workspace up to date with your repository.

- The book, *Java Tools for Extreme Programming: Mastering Open Source Tools Including Ant, JUnit, and Cactus* (Hightower and Lesiecki 2002), discusses how to use some of these tools.

# Private System Build

*Modern Times with Charlie Chaplin.*

A *Private Workspace (6)* allows you, as a developer, to insulate yourself from external changes to your environment. But your changes need to work with the rest of the system too. To verify this, you need to build the system consistently, including building with your changes. This pattern explains how you can check whether your code will still be consistent with the latest published code base when you submit your changes.

➤ *How do you verify that your changes do not break the build or the system before you check them in?*

In a development team with liberal codeline policies, changes happen very fast. You change existing code, add new modules to the codeline, and perhaps change the dependencies.

The only true test of whether changes are truly compatible is the centralized integration build. But checking in changes that are likely to break the build wastes time. Other developers will have you suffer through mistakes that you could have fixed quickly, and, unless the system build turnaround is very short, it will be harder for you to recall the source of an error because you may have lost the context in the meantime. Because the system build incorporates other changes as well as yours, as Figure 8–1 shows, it is the true test of whether your code integrates with the current state of the work. But this also makes it harder to isolate the source of problems.

At times your precheck-in build may work just fine, but the nightly build fails. Or your copy of the system that you get fresh from source control works just fine, but the product install made from the nightly build does not work

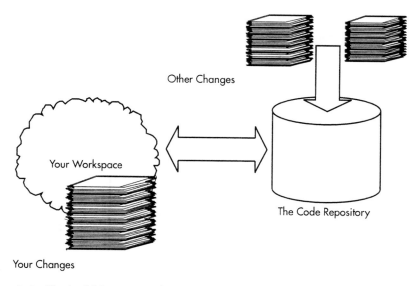

FIGURE 8–1.  The build integrates changes from everyone

the way you expect. You could always start debugging from a product install, analyzing logs and other runtime debugging facilities, but debugging from your development environment gives you more information. Sometimes the problem in this case is that the product build and install did not incorporate a new file or resource that you added to source control. Having release engineering maintain a list of what is built and installed adds a sense of reliability and reproducibility to the build, but if developers are the ones adding components to the version tree and they don't have visibility or control over what gets on the list, changing the build involves an added layer of communication, which implies an additional chance for error.

Often organizations have very well-established formal build procedures, but they don't scale down to the developers. Separate developer and release builds can make things simpler for some developers, but it also means that significant problems can't be found until the system build, which can be as infrequent as daily. This wastes time for anyone who needs a working code-line and makes it harder to get product release candidates to the testers.

To be able to do a reasonable test of the effect of the changes, you must be able to build all parts of the system that your code affects. This means building

## THE TWO TRUE WAYS

I was at a small company a while ago, and we had a fairly comprehensive set of build scripts and local build procedures. A developer could build the system and run tests on the local version simply by typing a few simple commands. This placed this company well ahead of organizations where there was no easy way to reproduce the effects of the nightly build. A few differences between the developer process and the release process caused us grief, however.

We were using CVS, which lets you define aliases for groups of directories, called modules. When you check out the files for a workspace, you check out one or more modules. Modules can depend on other modules, so checking out a module called "all," for example, gets you the entire source tree easily. I added a new directory to the CVS "all" module that all the developers used to create the workspace. The "Create a new workspace" script and build worked just fine.

The nightly build failed mysteriously. After much hand-wringing and some miscommunication, we discovered that the nightly build scripts didn't use the "all" module that the developers used, but it checked out each module one at a time. No one, aside from the release engineer, knew about this, and there was no semiautomatic mechanism to know that a change in a module required a change in the build script. We fixed this build error by sending an e-mail to the release engineer, but that approach doesn't scale well.

At another place, the installer that release engineering generated from the nightly build did not include the same versions of some components that developers were using. Debugging why an installed version didn't work and subsequently fixing it led to a culture of blame, and development felt that because they had little control over the process of creating install kits, solving the problem was out of their hands. By viewing the creation of an install kit as a process somewhat separate from building the software, getting a release out the door became harder.

components in your own workspace. You can work by patching your workspace with your built objects—for example, by building only the components you changed and altering the system PATH or CLASSPATH to use the new components first. But software systems are complicated, and you may not see the interactions of a "normal" build and execution process. Maintaining two procedures in parallel is difficult and error prone.

## THINK GLOBALLY BY BUILDING LOCALLY

> *Before making a submission to source control, build the system using a private system build similar to the nightly build.*

The private system build should have the following attributes.

*   Be like the *Integration Build (9)* and product builds as much as possible, although some details related to release and packaging can be omitted. It should at least use the same compiler, versions of external components, and directory structure.

*   Include all dependencies.

*   Include all the components dependent on the change (for example, various application executables).

The architecture will help you determine what is a sufficient set of components to build. An architecture that exhibits good encapsulation makes it easier to do this build with confidence. Figure 8–2 illustrates what goes into a build.

The build should not differ significantly from the nightly build. Wingerd and Seiwald suggest that "developers, test engineers, and release engineers should all use the same build tools" to avoid wasting time because you are not able to reproduce a problem (Wingerd and Seiwald 1998). In *The Pragmatic Programmer: From Journeyman to Master* (Hunt and Thomas 2000), Andy Hunt and Dave Thomas say, "If you do nothing else, make sure that every developer on a project compiles his or her software the same way, using the same tools, against the same set of dependencies. Make sure that the compilation process is automated."

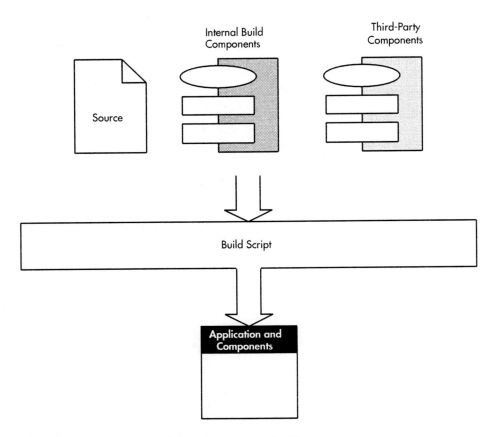

FIGURE 8–2.  Components of the private system build

If it must, it can differ from the product build in the following ways.

- It can be done in an IDE or other development environment as long as you know that the compiler is compatible with the one used in the product build process. Beware of differences that cause inconsistencies. And make an integration build script available to enable debugging.

- It can skip steps that insert identifying information into the final product—for example, updating version resources. Even steps like this can cause problems, so it is best to include these steps as well and just not check in changes that happen because of the build process. For example, if your changes did not change a version resource, do not commit the automatic change to the resource.

- It can skip some packaging steps, such as building installation packages, unless this is what the developer is trying to test.

It is important that the private build mechanism replicate the production build mechanism semantically as much as possible while still being usable by a single developer.

Examine how you decide what is put into the build and what is put into each component, such as a jar file or a library. Some common approaches follow.

- Build everything in version control. This has the advantage of making it easy to decide what to build and include. The disadvantage is that it can discourage developers from using the version control area to share files that may not yet be ready for use because, if they do not build, they can create errors. You still need to know how to package files into deliverable units.

- Build everything except items marked to exclude. This allows you to put anything in source control so that it is included by default but allows the option of excluding certain files.

- Build only parts of the version control tree that are explicitly included in a release list. The parts can be parts of a directory structure or individual files. The advantage of this approach is that it makes it easier to put experimental code into version control without worrying about breaking the build.

Either approach can work well. The build-everything approach is simpler. The include/exclude approach can work well if the include/exclude list is maintained in version control and can be built by developers, because the developers drive what code and components go into the product. As long as developers and the nightly build build the same files and "install" them in the same places, you will be able to debug problems easily. Any approach that has two different systems will cause conflict and delays.

When rebuilding in your workspace, you need to decide whether to do a full build or an incremental build. A full build is best to ensure that you are not missing any dependencies. But a full build may be impractical for active development because it can take a long time. So under most circumstances, you can do an incremental build if your dependencies are set up correctly. You should do a clean build under the following circumstances.

- When you are adding new files to the source control system. In this case, you also should start with an *empty* workspace. This is the only way to check that you added the file to the correct place. It's not unknown for people to forget to check in a file but for their builds and tests to pass because the file was in their workspace.

- When you make extensive changes involving key functionality. This may be overcautious but is best to do if you suspect that your dependency checking is in error.

You can also do a "clean" build of an individual component (for example, a library file or a jar).

They key thing to remember is that you should do this process repeatedly. Requiring a clean build all the time will make the process too slow to be useful, but never doing a clean build will expose you to any flaws in the way your tools handle dependency checking. An Integration Build should catch any problems of this sort, but the earlier you catch the problem, the less expensive it is to fix. When in doubt, do a clean build if time permits.

Once you have made sure that your code works in your current environment, update your workspace with the latest versions of code from the codeline you are working on, and repeat the build-and-test procedure.

A *Private System Build (8)* does take time, but this is time spent by only one person rather than each member of the team, should there be a problem. If building the entire system is prohibitive, build the smallest number of components that your changes affect.

If you change a component that other components depend on as an interface, it can become very difficult to cover every case. Ideally, you would build all clients. In this situation, let the *Smoke Test (13)* determine what executables to build.

As in many aspects of software development, this is a situation where communication is very helpful. If you think you will be making a sweeping change, run all the tests and then announce the pending change widely. This will enable people to let you know about their dependencies and to identify your change as a potential conflict if they see a problem later.

Related to the question of clean versus incremental build is the question of "what" to build. Start with whatever you need to run smoke tests. If you are developing a component that is used by one or more applications, consider building one or more of these executable applications. Ideally, you would build all the applications you know about. You don't need to be exhaustive though. If you miss something, your integration build and related testing will find it. This approach is not "passing the buck"; although each team member needs to attend to quality, everyone cannot take an infinite amount of time to do this. Consider the time in the release cycle, the reliability of your incremental build tools, and the time it takes for a full build.

Regardless of what approach you take daily, you should be able to start from an empty workspace and re-create the products of the nightly build when necessary.

## UNRESOLVED ISSUES

Once you know you can build the system, you still need to know whether you are breaking the functionality. To make sure the system still works, do a *Smoke Test (13)*. This pattern enables you to do a smoke test.

If the system is very large, it may not be efficient to build every component that uses your comoponents. These leftover dependencies will be validated in an *Integration Build (9)*.

What do you do when you find a build error in some other code that is related to your changes? Ideally, you should merge your own changes if you can identify them and they are not too extensive. If you change a widely used interface and the team has agreed to the change beforehand, it may make sense to communicate the timing of your change so that other team members can change the code they are responsible for. Your team dynamics will best decide the answer to this question.

## FURTHER READING

- Steve McConnell discusses the need to do a build before checking in code in *Rapid Development* (McConnell 1996).

- *The Pragmatic Programmer: From Journeyman to Master* (Hunt and Thomas 2000) has much good advice about build automation.

# 9

# Integration
# Build

*Making wiring assemblies at a junction box on the fire wall for the right engine of a B-25 bomber. North American Aviation, Inc. Inglewood, California, July 1942.*

All developers work in their own *Private Workspace (6)* so that they can control when they see other changes. This helps individual developers make progress, but in many workspaces people are making independent changes that must integrate together, and the whole system must build reliably. This pattern addresses mechanisms for helping ensure that the code for a system always builds.

≺ *How do you make sure that the code base always builds reliably?*

Because many people are making changes, it isn't possible for a lone developer to be 100 percent sure that the entire system will build after the changes are integrated into the mainline. Someone can be making a change in parallel with you that is incompatible with your change. Communication can help you avoid these situations, but problems still happen.

When you check in code changes, you may, despite your best intentions, introduce build errors. You may not need to build the entire code base before a check-in; there may be components that you don't know about or that are not part of another team's work. Your build environment may be inconsistent with the "release" build environment at any point. For example, if you work on a PC or a workstation, you may be slightly out of date with respect to the standard, in terms of compiler or operating system version or version for a third-party component. Or you may be trying out a new version of a component that seems compatible with the version everyone else is using. Duplicating your effort on multiple systems when the risks of a problem are small seems wasteful.

The best you can do is to try to build everything. A complete, clean build may take more time than you, or any other developer, can afford to spend. On the other hand, the time it takes for one person to do a complete build may be small compared with the time the team takes to resolve the problem; if you break the build, it will slow other people down. It is better to localize the problem as soon as you can. As Figure 9–1 shows, integration can be tricky, akin to putting puzzle pieces together.

A complete, centralized build may address some of these problems, but a centralized build works from checked-in code, so the damage is already done.

Some users of the system may not want, need, or be able to build the entire code base. If they are developing software that simply builds on top of another component, worrying about integration build issues will be a waste of their energy. They want a snapshot of the system that they know builds.

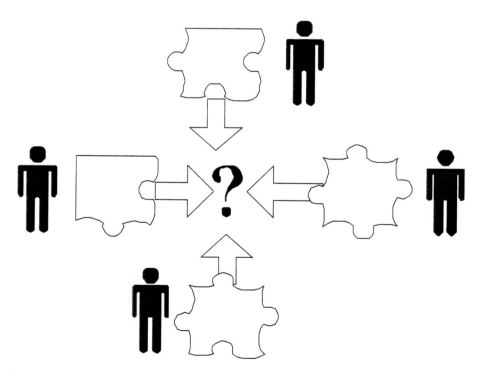

FIGURE 9–1. Integration can be difficult

## DEINTEGRATION BUILD

At a couple of start-ups I worked at, "builds" were done by individual developers and then "released" for testing. This caused a number of problems when the organization grew; different developers were experimenting with different versions of third-party components and compliers, which is reasonable if you want to minimize risk by exploring alternatives. But then when the build did not work or the built system didn't run, it was hard to figure out who was responsible because there was no one standard configuration or set of configurations that developers would run on their machines.

The fix was not to standardize development machines totally because that prevented experimentation. A build machine and a nightly build fixed the problems.

Tracking down inconsistent change sets is frustrating work for other developers, so the smoother the build, the higher the morale. You need a way to ensure that these inconsistencies are caught as quickly as possible, in an automated, centralized manner.

## DO A CENTRALIZED BUILD

> ✒ *Be sure that all changes (and their dependencies) are built using a central integration build process.*

This build process should be

• Reproducible.

• As close as possible to the final product build. Minor items, such as how files are version labeled might vary, but it is best if the integration build is the same as the product build. At the end of the integration build, you should have a candidate for testing.

- Automated or requiring minimal intervention to work. The harder a build is to run, the more even the best-intentioned teams will occasionally skip the process. If your source control system supports triggers, you could run the build on every check-in.

- A notification or logging mechanism to identify errors and inconsistencies. The sooner build errors are identified, the sooner they can be fixed. Also, rapid notification makes it easier to track the change that broke the build.

Having a centralized process simplifies integration, as Figure 9–2 shows. Perform the build in a workspace that contains the components being integrated. Determine how often to run the integration build based on the following factors:

- How long it takes to build the system

- How quickly changes are happening

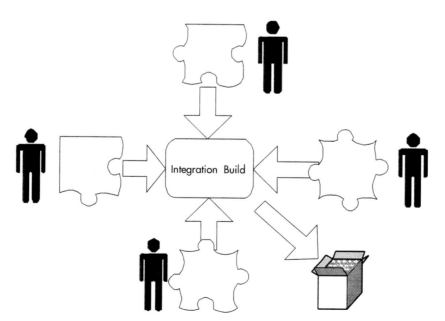

FIGURE 9–2. An integration build process assembles the pieces

If the system takes a long time to build or if the product is fairly static, consider at least a staged daily build, with an option to run additional builds as needed.

If the system can be built fairly quickly, consider running the build on every submission (check-in) to source control. Although this may seem resource intensive, it makes it very easy to determine the sequence of changes that broke the build. The trade-off is that if your version control system does not serialize changes adequately, you may have build failures simply because of inconsistencies.

Identify this build with a label in your version control system.

The integration build should be repeated on all supported platforms when the system supports them. Having individual developers do multiple builds can be a time sink.

Remember, the intent of the integration build is to catch build issues that fall through the cracks. Only if the builds fail consistently for the same reason should you add precheck-in verification steps.

If appropriate, use the integration build as the basis for an installation kit.

You check in a change to the repository. The source control system responds to the check-in by extracting all the files for the system, and it builds the resulting system. Errors in the build are reported to the build master as well as the person who submitted the change.

## UNRESOLVED ISSUES

Even if the system builds, it still may not work. Follow up the integration build with a *Smoke Test (13)* to ensure that the integration build is usable. If this build is to be published as a named stable baseline, also do a *Regression Test (15)*.

## FURTHER READING

- *Rapid Development* (McConnell 1996) describes a *Daily Build and Smoke Test (20)*.

- The *Daily Build and Smoke Test* pattern first appeared in Coplien's pattern language (Coplien 1995).

# 10

# Third Party Codeline

*Man who operates a small grocery store and second-hand furniture store in his home. Chanute, Kansas, November 1940.*

*Photo by John Vachon. Library of Congress, Prints & Photographs Division, FSA-OWI Collection, Reproduction Number: LC-USF34-061836-D.*

You want to focus on building the components for which you can add the most value, not on basic functionality that you can easily buy. Your codeline is associated with a set of external components that you will ship with your product. You may customize some of these to fit your needs. You need to associate versions of these components with your product. When you create your *Private Workspace (6)* or when you build a release for distribution, you need to associate these components with the version you are checking out. You also want your *Repository (7)* to contain the complete set of components that make up your system. This pattern shows how to track the third-party components in the same way you track your own code.

Y   *What is the most effective strategy to coordinate versions of vendor code with versions of product code?*

Using components developed by someone else means letting go of control of both the implementation and the release cycle for what could be a key building block of your system. The essence of source control and release management is the identification of what components go together to reconstruct a given version of a product. You still need to be able to reconstruct old builds for debugging and support, so you need a way to track which vendor release goes with which version of your code. If this were all your own code, you could simply label it in the version control system when you made a release. But vendor release cycles are different from your release cycles, as Figure 10–1 shows.

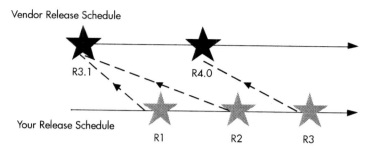

FIGURE 10–1. Vendor releases and your releases are not in sync

You need to identify easily which versions of third-party components go with which versions of your product. You could have a manifest or list to show this information.

Using a list to associate a vendor release with your product's version can be tricky during development. It is easy to use the third-party component's installation process if you are working with a static version, but in a dynamic environment, you should make installation with the correct version simple for developers. This can become complicated during development as well, because you need to coordinate third-party code versions with your code when you build a workspace, and you should be able to build and update a workspace automatically. Consulting a list and installing the right versions of components add an element of risk.

When you decided to use third-party code, it was because you wanted to save yourself work and because the third party added more value in a specific domain. Sometimes the outside code is not perfect and needs adaptations to work. You could be using publicly available code and need to customize it to fit your particular needs, or you might need to fix a bug in vendor code if you have access to the source. If you make custom changes to the vendor-provided code, you need to provide a way to integrate these changes into your subsequent releases until the vendor makes a release with the changes you need. In some cases, your changes may never be in the vendor release, and you need to reapply them to subsequent vendor releases.

Even with binary-only components that you do not change, you still need to associate releases of the outside code with releases of your product.

Using third-party code is, by its nature, risky, but treating third-party code as "outside" your system is risky if your system depends on it.

## A FEW STITCHES, TOO LATE

I've seen variations on the following scenario at a number of companies where I have worked. A company has a centralized build process that works fairly well. They use a number of third-party packages, and they handle version issues by using installation kits. When developers need to work on an older release, they use the installation kits. This works fine until they need to patch the third-party code. Then it is tricky to describe what custom version of the code goes with a point in the development cycle.

Another frequent issue is having difficulties debugging an old release that has been tracked down to the wrong version of a particular third-party component.

When people do their development against shared server systems, the problem becomes worse because there is a belief that only the server need be updated. This does not reflect the reality that they may need to fix a bug on an old version.

The problems have almost always been the result of a desire to avoid extra work to track the third-party code. As is often true, the short-term "savings" are more than lost in the long run.

## USE THE TOOLS YOU ALREADY HAVE

Y   *Create a codeline for third-party code. Build workspaces and installation kits from this codeline.*

Use your version control system to archive both the versions of the software you receive from the vendor and the versions you deliver to your customer. Use the branching facility of the version control system to track separate but parallel branches of development for the vendor's code and your customized versions of the vendor's code. When you get vendor code, make it the next version in the vendor branch and then merge the code from that branch into your customized branch. Your version control system should maintain enough information to build any version of your product using the correct versions of all components, internal and external.

What is "third-party code?" Third-party code is any code supplied by someone outside your organization or fixes and enhancements to that code. "Plug-ins" and extensions to a third-party framework are not third-party code and should be treated as product code. For example, if you have a library for parsing XML, that is third-party code. If you find that a version of the parser does not parse certain XML correctly, the fix for that should be made to the third-party codeline. Parsing event handlers that you write to use in your application are not part of the third-party codeline, though they certainly depend on the third-party code.

To accept vendor code, do the following.

1.  Add the vendor code to the appropriate directory of a vendor codeline. Add it to this codeline in exactly the way it unpacks from the distribution medium. If the component is something you can build, you should be able to build it from the checkout area.

2.  Label the check-in point with a label identifying the product and version.

3.  Immediately branch this new codeline. All the projects that will use this version of the vendor code will use the code from of the branch, making it possible to customize the code when the source is available. If you need to build the components locally, build them on this branch and check in the derived objects.

4.  Check in derived objects here to save time and effort; they should not change frequently.

5.  When a new vendor release appears, add it to the mainline portion of the vendor codeline. Branch again, and merge any relevant changes from the prior branch into the new branch.

Figure 10–2 shows the resulting codeline.

You can now easily reproduce prior versions of your own releases as well as those of the vendor. Customization differences can easily be isolated and

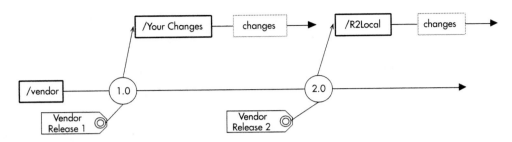

FIGURE 10–2.  Third-party codeline

reproduced so that you can see what you had to change for a given release. Differences between vendor releases can easily be isolated and reproduced to see what the vendor changed from release to release. By tracking customization changes on a separate branch from vendor changes, you are basically applying a divide-and-conquer approach of orthogonalization: Instead of one big change, you logically partition it into vendor changes and custom changes from a common base version. This reduces merge complexity. The resulting project version tree reflects the real-world development path relationships between the vendor and your group. This requires more storage space than simply keeping one source tree or one set (branch) of versions of the source tree. It also requires the oft-despised merging of parallel changes. Many feel that "merging is evil!" However, in this case, you are not the one who controls the development of the code. You are at the mercy of the third-party supplier for this. The best you can hope for is that they incorporate *all* your changes into their code base. Thus merging is unavoidable here.

When you release a version of your product, label the code that your product has been built and tested against on the third-party codeline with the same label as the product release.

Even if you make no changes to the vendor code, the release history is now traceable, and the vendor releases can be labeled with the appropriate product releases. Even if all you have access to are interface files (header files) and derived objects (libraries, jar files, and so on), track these using version control as well, even though the same amount of delta information is not available. If you do make changes, you should check in "compiled" versions of the product that include the changes. When you get a new vendor release, you can compare the source code in the various branches and consider doing a merge if your changes are not in the later release.

To create a developer workspace, make sure that you check out the third-party components that are part of the product check in. If your version control system supports the concept of sets of related parts of the source tree (that is, modules), when you check out a given point in time of your product, you get the appropriate version of the third-party component free. If your version control system allows you to rearrange the locations of objects during a check-in, check binary objects in to the appropriate common "bin" directory. Otherwise, be sure to alter PATHs and CLASSPATHs appropriately so that build and runtime environments point to the correct version.

Include the appropriate third-party product branches when labeling the release. For some components, you may have licensing constraints that say you must use the vendor installer. In this case, you still have traceability built into your version control system, and you know that what you are shipping matches what you are developing with. You may also be able simply to integrate the third-party code into your own installation process by placing binary objects in the same place as your product-specific code.

To reproduce a prior build, including the correct third-party code, check out the appropriate label into a new workspace, and have the correct versions of all components. For some software component systems, such as COM, you need to deal with systemwide registration of specific component versions.

If you have customized versions of build tools (for example, gcc) or if your product depends on a particular version of a particular tool, you can handle it by thinking about what you need to ship. If you need to ship all or part of the tool as a runtime component, use this approach. If the tool is used only at build time, you can still track it in your system using a third-party codeline, but dependencies between the tool version and the product version can be handled by flags and identifiers in makefiles, for example.

The procedures here apply to any runtime component—for example, language extensions to languages such as Perl, Python, or Tcl. The specific version of the interpreter environment is another story.

When you are using a dynamically loaded third-party component that is a shared resource that other products may use, you have to decide how to install it if it already exists on the target system. The options are to upgrade existing installations, require that your version be the correct one, or, if the component technology supports this, install the version you expect on the target system in addition to any existing versions. This may be tricky, for example, in the case of a COM component, where the vendor has not followed the appropriate version conventions. Because only one version of a COM component can be the latest, it may be impossible to have more than one installed. In other cases, you can install multiple versions by altering the PATH or CLASSPATH environment when you load your system. This is not so much a technical issue as a support and positioning issue. Having multiple copies means using more space, but running with a known version of a third-party component makes verification and testing easier.

Interpreted languages present a special case of this problem. If your system depends on a specific version of Python or Perl, you can install the additional version of the interpreter in a "special" path, or you can overwrite an existing installation, affecting all users of the product. Some of these tools allow you to build an executable that has an embedded interpreter, increasing isolation at the cost of a larger executable and less access to the source code, which eliminates a benefit of using a scripting language.

## UNRESOLVED ISSUES

If you are using a third-party product that is very stable or that you will never customize, you may not need to create a branch. The cost of the branch in this case is small, and it gives you the flexibility to make changes later, if you need to.

## FURTHER READING

Brian Berliner's 1990 paper, "CVS II: Parallelizing Software Development" (Berliner 1990), popularized the term "vendor branch" for this specific purpose.

# 11

# Task Level
# Commit

*Proud of his job. Smiling
worker in an eastern arsenal
hand finishes the interior
surface of a cradle for an
eight-inch gun, railway carriage. 1942.*

An *Integration Build (9)* is easier to debug if you know what went into it. This pattern discusses how to balance the needs for stability, speed, and atomicity.

> *How much work should you do between submissions to the version control system? How long should you wait before checking files in?*

When you make changes to the code base, you want to focus on the act of coding. Administrative tasks, such as checking in changes, precheck-in testing, and so on, are a distraction. Coding is a sequence of changes, bug fixes, and enhancements, and you need to track these changes. The revision history in your version control tool should reflect the way file changes map to functionality changes.

To add one feature or to fix one defect, you may need to make changes across many parts of the code base. But every change introduces a potential instability in the mainline. You would like to be able to roll back or remove a change if it causes unexpected problems. For this to work, changes need to be consistent and complete.

Depending on your *Codeline Policy (12)*, a check-in may involve a long sequence of steps, including testing, that will take time. You may want to avoid this overhead and delay checking in a change for as long as possible. For multiple feature changes that require changes to more than one module, it is certainly easier to make all the changes to a module at once. But the longer you are working on your own copy of the module, the more likely you may be in conflict with other people's changes, and the harder it will be to roll back a particular change.

When an integration build breaks, you want to be able to track down the change that broke it. A long list of changes in an integration build report is

112

## COARSE-GRAINED TASKS

We were working in an organization that had a very rigorous precheck-in validation process. As a result, developers would check in code, at most, once a day, occasionally less often. Because of this, each check-in would often mean more complicated merges (in the worst case) or failures that were hard to track down (the better case). Although the motivation was a reluctance to check things in, the deeper problem was that each check-in covered multiple tasks, so it was hard to say what the real source of a problem was and harder to roll back changes.

After enough of these situations, people started doing smaller-grained check-ins.

more work to process, but a more detailed change history makes it possible to remove selectively changes that may have broken the build.

It can be tricky to decide what a task-oriented change really is. Sometimes the definition of a task is natural. You may be fixing a problem that was assigned an issue number. If the issue can be fixed by changing one file, you have a natural atomic check-in. If a change spans multiple components across various systems, it is not obvious what changes go together unless they are checked in. If you err on the side of smaller units of work per check-in, you gain the overhead of processing the check-in. If you err on the side of larger-grained units of work, you lose the ability to back out small changes.

You want to be able to maintain a stable codeline and associate changes with features or defects that were fixed.

## DO ONE COMMIT PER SMALL-GRAINED TASK

> *Do one commit per small-grained, consistent task.*

Strive to have each commit of code changes reflect one task. This will enable you to make the most important changes first. The unit of work can be a new feature (or part), a problem report, or a refactoring task.

It is OK to batch changes if it makes sense and batching does not add significantly to the time that you are working on a local copy of the code. Consider the complexity of the task, how many files or components you need to change to implement the task, and how significantly the change will affect the system (how risky it is). Each change should represent a consistent state of the system.

Examples of reasonable change tasks are

- A problem report (a broad problem may have two or more check-ins associated with it)

- Changing calls to a deprecated method to use a new API for an entire system

- Changing calls to a deprecated method for a coherent part of the system

- A consistent set of changes that you accomplished in a day

When in doubt, err on the side of more check-ins because it is easier to roll back changes and see the effects of integration with other people's work. Also, because your revision control system is an indicator of the "pulse" of the development work, strive to check in changes at least once a day, if it makes sense.

Sometimes it makes sense to have a check-in for multiple defect reports or features. A degenerate example of this is a one- or two-line section of code that was responsible for numerous problem reports. In this circumstance, multiple check-ins would not be possible. But whenever you are changing separate parts of the code base, do one check-in per feature or defect report.

A precheck-in policy that is too vigorous can discourage this practice, so consider ways to streamline the precheck-in validation to test only what is necessary. Extended code freezes make it difficult to maintain this practice. Extended code freezes are bad for many reasons because they interrupt the flow of work.

Before you check in, be sure to catch up your workspace to the current state of the codeline and test for compatibilities.

## UNRESOLVED ISSUES

Some changes are far-reaching and inherently disruptive and long-lived. In this case, consider using a *Task Branch (19)*. If multiple people are working on a task branch, perform small-grained commits on the task branch.

Unit tests, smoke tests, and regression tests, as well as the edit policy, provide guidance on how to encourage small-grained check-ins.

Good integration between the development environment and the version control system will make the commit process fit in better with the flow of the developers' work.

# 12

# Codeline Policy

*Louise Thompson, daughter of a newspaper editor in Richwood. She is a printer's devil. Richwood, West Virginia, September 1942.*

*Photo by John Collier. Library of Congress, Prints & Photographs Division, FSA-OWI Collection, Reproduction Number: LC-USF34-084002-C.*

When you have multiple codelines, developers need to know how to treat each one. A *Release Line (17)* might have strict rules for how and when to check things in, but an *Active Development Line (5)* might have less strict rules. This pattern describes how to establish the rules for each codeline to suit its purpose.

> ✎ *How do the developers know which codeline to check their code in to, when to check it in, and what tests to run before check-in?*

Each codeline has a different purpose; one codeline might be intended for fixing bugs in a particular release; another codeline might be used for porting existing code to another platform; yet another is for day-to-day development. These codelines have different requirements for stability. If code is checked in to a codeline, ignoring the rules, productivity will suffer. Developers need to know which codeline they should be using and what the policies are on that codeline.

You can identify different codelines by their names. A codeline's name can tell you something about its purpose, but it can't express all the finer points of codeline usage, such as the policies. For example, a release line can be very restricted or only slightly slow, depending on the organization's strategy and vision. And it can be hard to come up with good, unambiguous naming conventions. Figure 12–1 shows how we might diagram the association between a codeline and a policy.

Once you decide how stable a codeline needs to be and how to realize that level of stability through processes, you need to inform developers of these

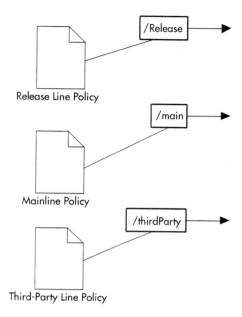

Release Line Policy

Mainline Policy

Third-Party Line Policy

FIGURE 12–1. Each codeline needs different rules

policies and then enforce them. You can provide formal documentation describing the finer points of codeline usage, but this requires extra effort for documentation and maintenance; once the documentation becomes out of sync with the policy, it is useless. Also, developers may perceive the formality of such a document as overbearing or as if it were some draconian tactic to interfere with "real work." It is easier for people to use a policy they understand and believe in than one that seems arbitrary (Karten 1994).

You want developers to behave properly and follow the policy, but even well-intentioned people forget things in the heat of a deadline. You can use peer pressure or punishment to enforce policies, but that can break down the team.

You can use automation to enforce policies, but it is hard to implement automated procedures correctly. Sometimes some steps in a process do not make sense, and it is hard to encode policies that allow you to skip a step. If you do provide a mechanism for sidetracking parts of the process, developers may ignore the process, from a well-intentioned sense of experience if nothing else.

For a codeline, different roles might have different degrees of leeway with executing the processes. For example, you may want to forbid permanently

**IMPEDANCE MISMATCH**

I worked at a software company that developed a number of products based on some common components. We were doing major work on one of the components, so at certain points in time interfaces were evolving or there might even be some bugs or inconsistencies. We were told that this was an evolving codeline and to develop accordingly. The other clients of the component were upset at having to adapt to changes, even though they were staged with plenty of warning.

The problem was that the codeline policy didn't mesh with the needs of all the users. There were a number of possible ways to address the problem. A stricter policy would have slowed progress. We could also have treated the other teams as external customers, providing them with "released" versions of the library.

deleting a file's history on a release line, but at times it makes sense, such as when someone checks in a new file accidentally. Someone needs to be able to fix this, or you will end up with useless files in your codeline. If you are too restrictive with permissions, you need to be able to give people permissions they need quickly. For example, if only the director of development can perform certain operations, but the director also travels much, you may be stuck. You may not be able to have an open codeline in all cases without having a free-for-all.

## DEFINE THE RULES OF THE ROAD

> *For each branch or codeline, formulate a policy that determines how and when developers should make changes. The policy should be concise and auditable.*

The codeline policy explicitly states the rudimentary policies an organization has about how to conduct concurrent development and how to manage releases. Vance says that "a codeline policy defines the rules governing the use of a codeline or branch" (Vance 1998). In addition to using naming conventions and meaningful codeline names, formulate a coherent purpose for each codeline. Describe the purpose in a clear and concise policy. The policy should be brief and should spell out the "rules of the road" for the codeline, including

- The kind of work encapsulated by the codeline, such as development, maintenance, or a specific release, function, or subsystem

- How and when elements should be checked in, checked out, branched, and merged

- Access restrictions for various individuals, roles, and groups

- Import/export relationships: the names of those codelines it expects to receive changes from and those codelines it needs to propagate changes to

- The duration of work or conditions for retiring the codeline

- The expected activity load and frequency of integration

Make the policy short and to the point: A good rule of thumb is one to three paragraphs, with one page as an absolute maximum.

Keep in mind that not all codeline policies require all the previous information. Specify only what is essential. Some version control tools allow you to associate a comment with each branch and codeline name. This is an ideal place to store the description of a suitably brief codeline policy. Developers can run a branch description for the codeline instead of digging around for its documentation. Otherwise, store the codeline policy in a well-known, readily accessible place. You could perhaps provide a simple command or macro that will quickly display the policy for a given codeline name.

You should create a branch whenever you have an incompatible policy. Some example of codeline policies follow.

- Development codeline—interim code changes may be checked in; affected components must be buildable (Wingerd and Seiwald 1998).

- Release codeline—software must build and pass regression tests before check-in; check-ins are limited to bug fixes; no new features or functionality may be checked in; after check-in, the branch is frozen until the entire QA cycle is completed (Wingerd and Seiwald 1998).

- Mainline—all components must compile and link, and pass regression tests; completed, tested new features may be checked in (Wingerd and Seiwald 1998).

Enforce parts of the policy by using any mechanism that your version control tool supports, such as triggers. If automatic enforcement becomes too constraining, use automation to report on adherence to the policy.

## UNRESOLVED ISSUES

To enforce a codeline policy effectively, you need to balance the utility of using automation and of the group's culture. You should look into your tools to see what mechanisms they provide. You can also consider using a tool such as ANT and write ANT tasks that enforce and audit your policies.

## FURTHER READING

- You can enforce codeline policies with the mechanisms in various tools. CVS, Perforce, ClearCase BitKeeper, and other tools support triggers that run before or after check-in. Tools such as ANT allow you to codify many build-related activities as tasks.

# 13

# Smoke Test

*Fighting fire of rice straw stack in rice field near Crowley, Louisiana, September 1938.*

*Photo by Russell Lee. Library of Congress, Prints & Photographs Division, FSA-OWI Collection, Reproduction Number: LC-USF33-011632-M3.*

An *Integration Build (9)* or a *Private System Build (8)* are useful for verifying build-time integration issues. But even if the code builds, you still need to check for runtime issues that can cause you grief later. This verification is essential if you want to maintain an *Active Development Line (5)*. This pattern addresses the decisions you need to make to validate a build.

Y   *How do you know that the system will still work after you make a change?*

You hope that you tested the code adequately before checking it in. The best way to do this is to run tests after every build and before you check something in to source control, but you need to decide which tests to run.

You can write tests that target the most critical or failure-prone parts of the code, but it is hard to develop complete tests.

You can play it safe and test everything you can think of, but it is time-consuming to run exhaustive tests, and your progress can be very slow. Also, if the test takes too long, you may lose focus and have a harder time correlating your recent changes with any problems. Long-running tests encourage larger-grained changes between testing. Unstructured and impromptu testing can help you discover new problems, but it may not have much of an effective yield.

Running detailed tests is time-consuming, but if you check in a change that breaks the system, you waste everyone's time. Rapid development and small-grained check-ins mean that you want the cost of precheck-in verification to be small.

## THE RIGHT BALANCE

Smoke tests are important on many levels. At one place I worked, release candidates were built periodically, and the first developer to try them had the pleasure of finding (and sometimes fixing) all the bugs. This led to people being reluctant to be the first to use the new builds and led to a fairly strong culture of blame.

At another place, the precheck-in test process was so exhaustive that developers feared it, and they did as few check-ins as possible, making many changes per check-in, thus not isolating changes. This had a negative effect on productivity. Also, it was very likely that someone would check in a conflicting change during the 60 minutes that the test ran. Running the long tests reduced productivity and quality.

The lessons here are that smoke tests are an essential precheck-in step and that more testing (precheck-in) is not always better.

## VERIFY BASIC FUNCTIONALITY

Y *Subject each build to a smoke test that verifies that the application has not broken in an obvious way.*

A smoke test should be good enough to catch "showstopper" defects but disregard trivial defects (McConnell 1996). The definition of "trivial" is up to the individual project, but you should realize that the goal of a smoke test is not the same as the goal of the overall quality assurance process.

The scope of the test need not be exhaustive. It should test basic functions and simple integration issues. Ideally, it should be automated so that there is little cost to do it. The *smoke test* should not replace deeper integration testing. A suite of unit tests can form the basis for the smoke test if nothing else is immediately available. Most important, these tests should be self-scoring. They should return a test status and not require manual intervention to see whether the test passed. An error may well involve some effort to discover the source, but discovering that there is an error should be automatic.

Running a smoke test with each build does not remove the responsibility for developers to test their changes before submitting them to the repository. Developers should run the smoke test manually before committing a change. A smoke test is most useful for bug fixes and for looking for inadvertent interactions between existing and new functionality. All code should be unit tested by the developer, and where reasonable, run through some scenarios in a system environment. A smoke test can also be run as part of the build process in concert with more thorough tests when the build is to be a release candidate.

When you add new basic functionality to a system, extend the smoke test to test this functionality as well. But do not put exhaustive tests that better belong in unit tests or regression tests.

*Daily Build and Smoke Test (20)* (Coplien 1995) describes the role of the smoke test in maintaining quality. Having a smoke test as part of a daily build is key to establishing *Named Stable Bases (20)*, which form the basis for workspaces.

A smoke test should

- Be quick to run, where "quick" depends on your specific situation

- Be self-scoring, as any automated test should be

- Provide broad coverage across the system that you care about

- Be runnable by developers as well as part of the quality assurance process

The hardest part about a self-scoring test is to determine input/output relationships among elements of a complex system. You don't want the testing and scoring infrastructure to be buggy. You want the test to work with realistic data exchanged between parts of the system.

To get meaningful results from a smoke test, you need to work from a consistent build. A *Private System Build (8)* lets you build the system in a way that will give meaningful test results.

Canned inputs are fine as long as they are realistic enough. If your testing infrastructure is too complicated, you add risks around testing the test.

If the quality goals are such that you need to do exhaustive testing, consider using *Task Branch (19)*, or have a different codeline policy. Also consider branching release lines.

A smoke test is an end-to-end test, more black box than white box.

## UNRESOLVED ISSUES

A smoke test does leave gaps that should be filled by a more thorough QA procedure and *Regression Test (15)* suite to do more exhaustive testing to identify degradation in behavior. Developers should also develop a *Unit Test (14)* for every module they need. Use a *Unit Test (14)* to verify that the module you are changing still works adequately before you check in the change.

The trade-off we need to make involves the speed of check-in versus the thoroughness of the test. The longer the precheck-in test, the longer the check-in. Longer check-ins may encourage developers to have larger-granularity commits. This goes against an important goal of using version control.

## FURTHER READING

- *Rapid Development* (McConnell 1996) has some good advice on various testing strategies, including the trade-offs between completeness and speed.

- The *Mythical Man-Month* (Brooks 1995) also has advice on making these trade-offs, and it is a classic book that every software developer should read.

# 14

# Unit Test

All the parts of an airplane engine, which has just undergone severe tests in a Midwest plant, are spread out for minute inspection. Continental Motors, Michigan, February 1942.

Photo by Alfred T. Palmer. Library of Congress, Prints & Photographs Division, FSA-OWI Collection, Reproduction Number: LC-USE6-D-005032.

Sometimes a *Smoke Test (13)* is not enough to test a change in detail when you are working on a module, especially when you are working on new code. This pattern shows you how to test detailed changes so that you can ensure the quality of your codeline.

➤ *How do you test whether a module still works as it should after you make a change?*

Checking that a class, module, or function still works after you make a change is a basic procedure that will help you maintain stability in your software development. It is also easier to understand what can go wrong at a low-level interface than it is at a system level. On the other hand, testing small-scale units all the time can become tedious.

Integration is where most of the problems become visible, but when you have the results of a failed integration test, you are still left with the question, What broke? Also, testing integration-level functions can take longer to set up because they require many pieces of the system to be stable. You want to be able to see whether any incremental change to your code broke something, so being able to run the tests as often as you like has benefits. You also want to run comprehensive tests on the item you are changing before check-in.

Since a smoke test is by its nature somewhat superficial, you want to be able to ensure that each part of a system works reasonably well. When a system test or a smoke test fails, you want to figure out what part of the system broke. You want to be able to run quick tests in development to see the effect of a change. Additional testing layers add time. Tests that are too complex take more effort to debug than the value they add is worth.

## SAFETY FIRST

I'd worked at a number of places where testing was a bit ad hoc. We did system tests but never focused on unit tests. When system tests failed, we'd run code through the debugger, and sometimes we'd find a problem. Other times, we'd find that the problem was that a client violated an interface contract. It took more effort than we needed to spend. After the XP book came out, and having been inspired by chatting with Kent Beck and Martin Fowler at OOPSLA, I took unit testing a bit more seriously.

On the next project, my colleagues and I wrote unit tests using the CPPUnit framework. It took some effort to convince them of the value, but when we started to isolate problems quickly (often to parts of the code that did not have unit tests!), my colleagues became convinced. Not only that, but the unit tests made code changes less scary.

We want to isolate integration issues from local changes, and we want to test the contracts that each element provides locally.

## TEST THE CONTRACT

*Develop and run unit tests.*

A unit test tests fine-grained elements of a component to see that they obey their contract. A good unit test has the following properties (Beck 2000).

* It is automatic and self-evaluating. A unit test can report a boolean result automatically. A user should not have to look at the detailed test results unless there is an error.

* It is fine-grained. Any significant interface method on a class should test using known inputs. It is not necessary to write tests to verify trivial methods such as accessors and setters. To put it simply, the test tests things that might break.

- It is isolated. A unit test does not interact with other tests. Otherwise, one test that fails may cause others to fail.

- It tests the contract. The test should be self-contained so that external changes do not affect the results. If an external interface changes, you should update the test to reflect this.

- It is simple to run. You should be able to run a unit test by using a simple command line or a graphical tool. No setup should be involved.

You should run unit tests

- While you are coding

- Just before checking in a change and after updating your code to the current version

You can also run all your unit tests when you are trying to find a problem with a smoke test or a regression test, or in response to a user problem report.

Try to use a testing framework such as JUnit (or CppUnit, PyUnit, and other derived frameworks). This will enable you to focus on the unit tests and not distract yourself with testing infrastructure.

Unit testing is indispensable when making changes to the structure of the code that should not affect behavior, such as when you are refactoring (Fowler 1999).

Grady Booch in *Object Solutions* suggests that during evolution you carry out unit testing of all new classes and objects but also apply regression testing to each new complete release (Booch 1996).

I've found that if I can't come up with a good unit test for a class or set of classes, I should make sure that my design is not overly complicated and not too abstract.

## UNRESOLVED ISSUES

Writing unit tests can be tedious. You should try to use a framework such as JUnit to simplify some of the tedious parts of writing test cases.

If your public interface is narrow, but you want to test other functions, you need to decide whether to open your interface to allow for testing or do something else. There are a number of approaches to this problem.

## FURTHER READING

- Unit testing is a key part of Extreme Programming (Beck 2000; Jeffries et al. 2000).

- To simplify your testing, try the testing framework JUnit (http://www. junit.org) for Java programming and the related frameworks for many other languages, available at http://www.xprogramming.com.

- *The Art of Software Testing,* by Glen Meyers (Myers 1979), is a classic book on testing and has a good discussion on black-box versus white-box testing. The book is based on work on mainframe systems, but it is still useful.

15

# Regression
# Test

*An experimental scale model of the B-25 plane is prepared for wind tunnel tests in the Inglewood, California, plant of North American Aviation, Inc. October 1942.*

*Photo by Alfred T. Palmer. Library of Congress, Prints & Photographs Division, FSA-OWI Collection, Reproduction Number: LC-USE6-D-007389.*

135

A *Smoke Test (13)* is quick but not exhaustive. For it to be effective, you need to do the hard work of exhaustive testing as well. If you want to establish release candidates, you need to be sure that the code base is robust. This pattern explains how to generate builds that are no worse than the last build.

> *How do you ensure that existing code doesn't get worse as you make other improvements?*

Software systems are complex, and with each change or enhancement to a system comes the possibility of breaking something seemingly unrelated to your changes. Fixing a defect has a substantial chance of introducing another (Brooks 1995). Without change, you can't make progress, but the impact of a change is hard to measure, especially in terms of how a unit of code interacts with the rest of the system.

You can exhaustively test your system after each build. Exhaustive testing takes time, but if you don't do this testing, you waste developer and perhaps customer time. If everyone runs exhaustive tests all the time, they will not be able to spend much time coding.

Even if you decide to do exhaustive system-level testing periodically on the code base, you are left with the problem of how to structure the tests. You can write tests from first principles by analyzing the inputs and outputs, but the payoff for writing tests like this on a system level may be small relative to the effort they take to write. You can also make intelligent guesses about what to test, but a software system is always full of surprises, especially in the ways it can fail.

When you solve the problem of which system tests to execute, you are still left with the problem of when to run them. Some integration tests may need resources that are not on every development machine. What is a good development environment may not always be the best test of the system. Reproducing some problems may require large data sets or multiple clients in a client-server system. You may not have the resources to run these sorts of tests all the time.

When the system does break, you want to identify the point in time when something broke. If you run the tests on every build or check-in to source control, you will be able to identify when something failed. But your testing may not keep up with your check-in and build process if the tests take long enough.

If your exhaustive tests find a problem and you fix it, you want to be sure that you can identify when this problem happens again because you don't want to waste time on known issues. A problem that happens once can happen again (this is what we mean by regression, after all). This means that we should accumulate a set of test cases as we discover problems, especially because we may not be able to guess all the problems ahead of time. These test cases can add up over time.

We need to be able to check for these recurring failure modes.

## TWO STEPS BACK

I worked for a small software product company that had a code base combined of newer, cleaner code and code that evolved. On any given day, it was not clear whether you could get an update from source control and have a working system or you would have to spend the day getting the system to a point where you could do your work. The problem was that there was no automated testing of the core APIs. People would avoid moving to a current code base in fear of wasting a day, but this eventually caused other problems.

The lack of a way to check for old problems recurring caused many easily preventable quality issues.

## TEST FOR CHANGES

> ➤ *Run regression tests on the system whenever you want to ensure stability of the codeline, such as before you release a build or before a particularly risky change. Create the regression tests from test cases the system has failed in the past.*

Regression tests are end-to-end black-box tests that cover actual past or anticipated failure modes. A regression test can identify a system-level failure in the code base but may not necessarily identify what broke. When a regression test fails, debugging and unit tests may be necessary to determine what low-level component or interface broke.

Regression tests test changes in integration behavior. They are large-grained and test for unexpected consequences of integrating software components. Unit tests can be thought through fairly easily. As you add component interactions, it is harder to write tests based on first principles.

Build regression test cases from

- Problems that you find in the prerelease QA process

- Customer- and user-reported problems

- System-level tests based on requirements

As you discover problems, write a test that reproduces the problem and add that scenario to the test. Over time you will end up with a large suite of tests that covers your most likely problem areas. Each problem may involve more than one test case. You can include running all unit tests in your regression testing, but it is better if the tests involve system input.

Regression testing is designed to make sure that the software has not taken a step backward (or regressed). Always run the same tests for each regression cycle. Add tests as you find more conditions or problematic items to test. Always add test cases to the regression test suite; if a problem happened once, it is likely to happen again, so remove test cases only for very well thought-through reasons.

Because regression tests can take a long time to run, you don't want to run them before every check-in or even after every build (unless resources permit). There are advantages, however, to having an automated procedure to run the regression test after each change so that you can identify the point at which the system regressed. Run the regression tests as part of the nightly build. Developers should also run a regression test before any significant sweeping change. If something breaks, you can always run the unit tests to localize the change. You also have to investigate if the unit test inputs no longer match the system. Institute a policy of automated regression testing tied to each release (Booch 1996).

## FURTHER READING

- Steve McConnell has a lot of information about testing of all kinds in *Code Complete* (McConnell 1993).

- *The Art of Software Testing*, by Glen Myers (Myers 1979), is a classic.

# 16

# Private Versions

*"Morgue" of the New York Times newspaper. Clippings on every conceivable subject are filed here for a reference. Editors and writers phone in for information. New York, September 1942.*

*Photo by Marjory Collins. Library of Congress, Prints & Photographs Division, FSA-OWI Collection, Reproduction Number: LC-USW3-009019-D.*

Sometimes you want to evaluate rapidly a complex change that may break the system while you maintain an *Active Development Line (5)*. This pattern describes how to maintain local traceability without affecting global history unintentionally.

➤ *How can you experiment with a complex change and benefit from the version control system without making the change public?*

Some programming tasks are best done in small, retractable steps. If you are making a complex change, you may want to *checkpoint* an intermediate step so that you can back out of a change easily. For example, if there are a number of design choice points, you may want to explore one path and be able to back out to an earlier decision point when you see a problem with the implementation, as shown in Figure 16–1.

Your version control system provides a way of checkpointing your work and reverting to earlier states of the system. When you check something in to the active codeline, you subject every other member of your team to the changes. When you are exploring implementations, you may not want to share your choices until you have fully evaluated them. You may even decide that the change was a dead end.

If you don't want to use the version control system to track your changes and not cause other developers delay, you will have to test your changes in accordance with your codeline policy. You may also need to integrate changes so that other code works with any API changes you made. This can take an unjustifiably long time if you are just experimenting with options. If

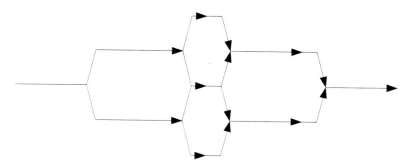

FIGURE 16–1. Each decision leads to more choices, until you pick the solution

you decide to skip the tests, you will cause problems for other developers if you break the build or the built system. If you skip integrating your changes with the rest of the system, you will break the codeline. This is too much work for a change that you may throw away in an hour or a day. Figure 16–2 shows still another option; you can check in changes and revert at each step. This generates many superfluous change events for the rest of the team and enables you to retrace your changes only one step at a time.

Even if you did put the effort into validating changes before checking them in, you would be cluttering the version history with changes that are not salient to the main change path. Because the version history for a component is important, it may be important to keep the version history uncluttered with insignificant changes.

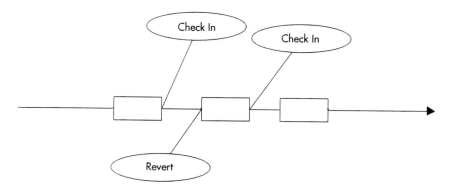

FIGURE 16–2. Using the codeline for staging generates a lot of noise

**USE CAUTION**

Being able to use version control without publishing changes is one of the things that you miss only when you don't have it. When the practice isn't established, people often avoid the issue entirely. The times that I've seen this used in practice are in situations involving major refactorings or when developing proof of concepts.

Being able to roll back bad ideas before everyone sees them is very helpful.

You might consider just doing all the changes in your workspace and not checking in any intermediate work. If you don't check in any changes, you can't back off changes. You can take an ad hoc approach to saving the state of your work at various points in time by copying files or using some other mechanism, but then you are really creating a minimalist version control system. It's optimistic to expect to develop a mechanism that gives you the features you want reliably without investing more work than is appropriate.

You can also use private versions to test how integrating with the current state of the codeline will work with your software. You can check your changes in to your private version, then catch up with the codeline, and then easily roll back if there is a problem.

The dilemma is that you want to use the tools of your trade, including version control, to create a stable, useful codeline, but you want to do this privately.

## A PRIVATE HISTORY

> ⟫ *Provide developers with a mechanism for checkpointing changes at a granularity they are comfortable with. This can be provided by a local revision control area. Only stable code sets are checked in to the project repository.*

Set up developers' workspaces so that they can check in changes to a non-public area when they are making an appropriate change. The mechanism should allow them also to integrate their working code base with the current state of the active development line. This private repository should use the same mechanisms as the usual version control system so that the developers do not need to learn a new mechanism. This allows developers to experiment with complex changes to the code base in small steps, without breaking the codeline if an experiment goes awry. Developers can make small steps with confidence, knowing that they can abandon part of a change if it takes longer than they expect.

There are many ways to implement this. One way is to have an entire *Private Workspace (6)* dedicated to a task. This is appropriate when you want to experiment with a global change (for example, to an interface) and evaluate the consequences of the change to see whether they are manageable in the time you have. If your change involves only a small portion of the source tree (one Java package or one directory), you can map that part of the workspace to a "private" repository—for example, a local CVS repository or a developer-specific branch of the main repository that is not integrated with the active line. You then redirect certain check-ins to the private repository. When you are done with your work, check the files in to the main repository, either by specifying the repository or by copying files from the test workspace to your real one. Be sure to follow all the procedures in your standard codeline policy before checking the code in to the active codeline.

Some tools provide for promotion levels or stages. You can create private stages to use version control and not publish changes to the rest of the team.

It is important to make sure that developers using private versioning remember to migrate changes to the shared version control system at reasonable intervals. Although one way to implement this is to provide a separate source control repository for each developer in addition to the shared repository, this can also be implemented within the framework of the existing revision control system. If the revision control mechanism provides a means for restricting access to checked-in versions that are not yet ready for use by others, we can use the common version control system as a virtual private repository.

The important principle is to allow developers to use the version control system to checkpoint changes in a granularity that meet their needs, without any risk of the changes (which may be inconsistent) being available to anyone else.

# 17

# Release
# Line

*Freight operations on the Chicago
and Northwestern Railroad
between Chicago and Clinton,
Iowa. The rear brakeman signals
the engineer to test the brakes by
applying and releasing them. This is
the signal for "apply." January 1943.*

*Photo by Jack Delano. Library of Congress,
Prints & Photographs Division, FSA-OWI Collection,
Reproduction Number: LC-USW3-014014-E.*

You want to maintain an *Active Development Line (5)*. You have released versions that need maintenance and enhancements, and you want to keep the released code base stable. This pattern shows you how to isolate released versions from current development.

> ⤴ *How do you do maintenance on released versions without interfering with your current development work?*

Once you release a version of a product or component, it may need to evolve independently of your primary development. Although it might be ideal from your perspective for your customers simply to update to new releases to get bug fixes, the reality is that in many circumstances you need to make a fix based on the already shipped version of the codeline. You may need to fix an urgent problem, and the new release will not be ready in time. If your application has data migration or a complicated deployment process for it, your customers may not be willing or able to upgrade immediately. You are often faced with the problem of how to conduct development of a future release while at the same time responding in a timely manner to all the many bug reports and enhancement requests that are inevitably going to be logged against the active development.

You need to identify what code was part of the release and what code is in the main development stream. One way to identify what is in a release is by labeling the release in the current codeline, shipping that snapshot, and then continuing to work on the mainline. Figure 17–1 illustrates this approach. Doing things this way does not allow you to fix something in a

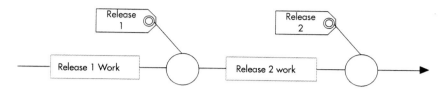

FIGURE 17–1. Doing all your work on the mainline

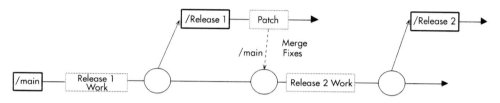

FIGURE 17–2. Create a branch when you ship

released product independently of the mainline. Although you need to fix bugs on released products, the current development line may be evolving in a direction that is quite different from the soon to be delivered release, and it may not be easy to deliver a fix quickly.

You can create a branch when the product ships to isolate the release line from current work. Then if there are fixes that apply to both the branch and the mainline, you need to merge the changes or duplicate the work. Figure 17–2 shows this situation.

You can put your new work on a branch and ship the mainline. You then can merge back. This means that most developers need to merge their work; hopefully, the released code won't change too much over time. You may have more than one customer, each with variations of the released software; you may need to keep track of multiple releases that are derived from other releases. You can model this by using the staircase structure shown in Figure 17–3. This structure makes it very hard to figure out what code is common among the releases.

You can try to keep customers on only major releases. Critical bug fixes and enhancements need to be effected immediately, often well before the next major release is ready to ship.

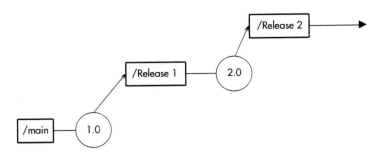

FIGURE 17–3. Staircase of dependent branches

The maintenance effort (bug fixes and enhancements) in the current release may be incompatible with some of the functionality or refactoring already implemented in the next release.

## LINEAR DEVELOPMENT

Mainline-only development has a number of advantages. It reduces complexity and redundant effort. Some early-stage companies work closely enough with their few customers that they can focus development on what these customers need, and bug fixes are simply additions to the codeline. You can label each release point and then have your customers move to the new release. They'll probably get some additional features, so they won't mind, and all your work may be short-term enough that you'll always be able to ship your code.

With success and planning comes a circumstance where the main codeline might not always be shippable because the infrastructure needed to support a new feature might not be ready until after the code is ready. Also, with more than one customer, you may not be able to get your customer base to upgrade at the same time.

You need a way to get released code evolve independently of mainline code so that you can do bug fixes.

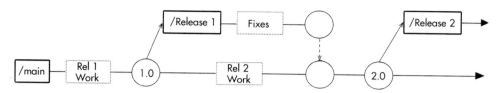

Figure 17–4.  Release line

## BRANCH BEFORE RELEASING

> ✑ *Split maintenance/release and active development into separate codelines. Keep each released version on a release line. Allow the line to progress on its own for bug fixes. Branch each release from mainline.*

Rather than trying to accommodate maintenance of the current release and development of the next release in the same codeline, split maintenance and development into separate codelines. All bug fixes and enhancements to the current release take place in the maintenance line, and effort for the next major release takes place in the development line. Ensure that changes in the maintenance line are propagated to the active development line regularly. Figure 17–4 shows this structure.

Propagate bug fixes from the mainline to the release line where possible. Once the mainline has progressed, you may still be making changes to the released line; code on the release line becomes dead-end code when that release is no longer supported.

When you are ready to ship, label the code on the mainline, and branch. Fix any errors on the released codeline on the branch, and merge any relevant changes back into the mainline before the next release. All work for future releases goes on the mainline.

At release time, branch all code, including third-party code.

## FURTHER READING

- "Streamed Lines" (Appleton et al. 1998) describes more branching patterns.

- *Software Release Methodology*, by Michael Bays (Bays 1999), discusses various types of codelines.

# 18

# Release-Prep Code Line

*Train pulling out of a freight house at a Chicago and Northwestern Railroad yard. The wooden trestle is part of a long chain belt used to carry blocks of ice from the ice house to the freight house. Chicago, Illinois. December 1942.*

You're finishing up a release and also need to start development on the next release. You want to maintain an *Active Development Line (5)*.

Y  *How do you stabilize a codeline for an impending release while also allowing new work to continue on an active codeline?*

Before a release is ready to ship, there is often much work to do to get the active development line shippable. There are last-minute bugs to fix and last-minute details related to installation to tend to, packaging, and so on. It is best not to do any major new work on the active development codeline while this cleanup is going on because you don't want to introduce any new problems. You should have very restrictive check-in and QA policies during this cleanup period.

One solution is to freeze development on the active development line until the release stabilizes. You can institute a strict policy that only essential changes are made to the codeline. If things go well, this may take only a day or so. But the stabilization work may involve part of the team, and there is new work to do for the next release, so you do not want to stop work at all. If the code freeze lasts longer than this, it is very wasteful of resources and frustrating to developers who are doing new work because they will have to work without the version control system. If people work on the changes without checking them in to the version control stream, you lose all the benefits of having a version control system and put yourself at risk of having chaos when the freeze is lifted.

Another possible solution is to branch the codeline into a release codeline and do all your work on the branch. If you branch too early, you will have to

## IDLE HANDS

Lots of places I've worked have instituted code freezes before releases. This is a good idea in principle, but when the code freeze lasts for days or weeks, it seems like less of a good idea. The stated reason for freezing instead of doing something that allows parallel work is that it is less work. Of course, it adds frustration and delays the release.

I've seen this so many times, often at the same time that there is lots of pressure to deliver code. Version control tools offer the ability to allow concurrent work, but they aren't used often or well.

do a lot of merging between the release line and the mainline. Branching gives you isolation but at the expense of added work in doing merges.

Developers want to get work done and avoid merges. Management wants the current code to be stable.

## BRANCH INSTEAD OF FREEZE

- *Create a release engineering branch when code is approaching release quality. Finish the release on this branch, and leave the mainline for active development. The branch becomes the release branch.*

You mark the release of a product with a branch. Instead of branching immediately *after* release, branch before the release. This enables you to branch instead of freeze. Instead of freezing the main codeline during release engineering activities, create a separate line for release integration and engineering, and allow other development to continue on the development line.

Create the release engineering line when the code is approaching stability. The closer to "done" code you create the branch, the less merging you will have to do between this line and the mainline. The trade-off is that if you wait longer, you may find yourself in a code-freeze situation.

This anti-freeze (release engineering) line becomes the release maintenance line after a successful release. It still serves the same purpose of "sync

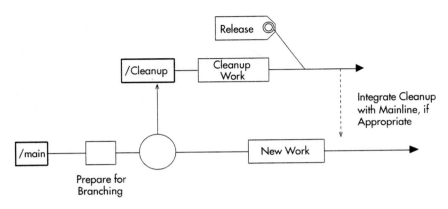

FIGURE 18–1.  Release-Prep Code Line

and stabilize," but now it is an ongoing effort that continues even after the release.

In reality, there may be a small "freeze" window—as long as it takes to create a consistent branch. If you can avoid this, all the better, but even if your "freeze" is short, you are still ahead of where you were when you had to freeze until you ship and release. Figure 18–1 illustrates this structure.

Changes can take place in each of the two codelines at the appropriate pace. Critical fixes and enhancements can be implemented and delivered without immediately impeding future development. Maintenance releases or "patches" can be periodically released without severely impacting development on the next release. The codeline owner of the development line can set a policy for how and when changes are propagated from the maintenance line to the development.

## UNRESOLVED ISSUES

If only a few people are working on the next release, instead of starting a release-prep branch, start a *Task Branch (19)* for the new work.

To keep the codeline in good shape while you are doing a potentially disruptive task, consider using a *Task Branch (19)*. This pattern forms the basis for a *Release Line (17)*.

# Task
# Branch

*Montour no. 4 mine of the Pittsburgh Coal Company. There are miles and miles of track in a mine, and the maintenance of the roadbed, ballast, and switches keeps a crew working constantly. Pittsburgh, Pennsylvania (vicinity), November 1942.*

*Photo by John Collier. Library of Congress, Prints & Photographs Division, FSA-OWI Collection, Reproduction Number: LC-USW3-010723-C.*

## HANDLING LONG-LIVED TASKS

Some development tasks take a long time to implement, and intermediate steps are potentially disruptive to an *Active Development Line (5)*. This pattern describes how to reconcile long-term tasks with an active development line.

≫ *How can your team make multiple, long-term, overlapping changes to a codeline without compromising its consistency and integrity?*

You usually want to use the version control system as a mechanism to keep the entire team up to date on what everyone is doing. Under normal circumstances, you will check in changes frequently. Some development tasks should not be integrated into the mainline to share with the rest of the team until they are complete. For example, you may be making a major change to an interface, and you need to be sure it works before you publish it to the team.

When you are doing parallel development without controlling the interaction between everyone's concurrent changes, you can end up with wasted effort and rework. Most of the time, you want to use the version control system as your communications mechanism. You want to share your work with everyone as soon as you think it is ready because frequent integration is a good way to improve global stability. You also want to put your changes into version control as soon as is reasonable to ensure that you have traceability and recoverability. Also, on a practical note, development systems often do not have the same backup and

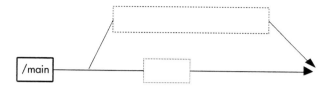

FIGURE 19–1. Some tasks are for the future.

recovery infrastructure around them as the disk drives that contain the version control software.

Some changes would destabilize the active codeline if you checked them in. For example, a major refactoring can't easily be done in stages, yet you don't want to wait a week before checking in the complete set of changes. Also, because your version control system is a good mechanism for communicating changes to other developers who are working on the same task, you need a place to check your code in to. The alternatives, which include sharing files and other mechanisms that bypass the version control system, can easily cause you to be out of synchronization with each other, even if your communication is good, which is often not the case because we are distracted. Figure 19–1 illustrates this concept.

Another example of a situation where a small group of developers is working on a task that can cause conflict is this: You are approaching a product release, but a small part of your development team is working on a

## PARALLEL LINES

We were changing the persistence mechanism for our application. This had far-reaching implications. We were changing the mechanism because there were problems with the existing one, so bug fixes were going on as well. The fact that there was some isolation at the module level between the persistence code and the other parts of the system made this a bit easier.

By creating a branch with the files we were updating, we could enable a group of people to enhance the persistence mechanism while other work was going on.

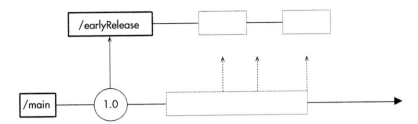

FIGURE 19–2.  Creating a release line too early is troublesome.

new feature for a subsequent release. You want this subset of your team to share code changes by using some sort of version control system, but the changes cannot go into the active development line because they are not for this release. If only a small part of the team is working on these changes, the overhead of creating a release line might be too great, because everyone is doing work on the release line, and the mainline should remain in sync with it. With some tools, the only reliable way to synchronize both lines is to check code in to both places. Figure 19–2 illustrates this.

A small team of developers working on a future task can have a more lax codeline policy for keeping their work synchronized with the active mainline because they can communicate among themselves more efficiently than the larger team can.

You need a way to allow a team of developers to work on a task that is parallel to the mainline for a short time, while keeping all the benefits of the version control tools.

## USE BRANCHES FOR ISOLATION

> *Fork off a separate branch for each activity that has significant changes for a codeline.*

A branch is a mechanism for reducing risk. You can use a task branch as "a mechanism for physically isolating riskier development ventures from the code base" (Vance 1998). Once the activity is complete and all its file changes have been tested, check in files on the activity branch. When the task is complete, merge with the mainline. Michael Bays describes the scenario for a task branch (though not calling it by that name).

> It is common for a single developer to create a branch from the trunk in order to execute a change that will require a nontrivial amount of time and not be impeded by changes others are making in the same files. As work in this developer branch continues, the source trunk will continue to iterate through revisions with the work of others. Eventually, the developer will want to take the files that she has changed and merge them back into the latest file versions on the trunk (Bays 1999).

You need to be sure that all the code that has changed on the mainline since the time you started your branch still works with yours. Merge the activity branch into the appropriate codeline (as a single transaction). Otherwise, notify the appropriate codeline owner that the change is complete and ready to be merged, and provide the codeline owner with any other necessary information for finding, merging, and testing the change task.

If your version control system supports "lazy branching," where your branch inherits all the code from the mainline unless it changed on the branch, you can use a task branch when you have to isolate a small amount of "future work" from the mainline. Figure 19–3 shows this structure.

Task branches are especially useful when you have multiple people sharing work that needs to be integrated together. For this reason, you can also use a task branch for integration before releasing a change to the active development line. You can integrate a number of changes into the task branch and then

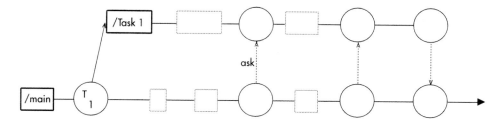

FIGURE 19–3. Task branch

merge the task branch back into the active development line when the changes pass your tests.

It is important to integrate changes from the active development line into the task branch frequently. You want the final integration of the task branch with the active codeline to go as smoothly as possible.

# Referenced Patterns

*1790s English-style barn. Union, Maine. October 2001.*

*Photo by Stephen P. Berczuk, © 2001.*

This chapter provides a brief summary of patterns from other sources that we reference in this book.

## NAMED STABLE BASES

This pattern was originally published in "A Generative Development Process Pattern Language" (Coplien 1995).

Intent: How frequently do you integrate? Stabilize system interfaces no more than once a week. Other software can be changed and integrated more frequently (summary is from *The Pattern Almanac 2000* (Rising 2000)).

## DAILY BUILD AND SMOKE TEST

This pattern was originally published in "A Generative Development Process Pattern Language" (Coplien 1995).

Intent: How do you keep the changes from getting out of hand and contain the potential for errors in the build? At least daily, build the software, and perform a smoke test to determine that the software is still usable.

Appendix A

# SCM Resources Online

This section describes some useful SCM resources available on the World Wide Web.

## THE CONFIGURATION MANAGEMENT YELLOW PAGES

- http://www.cmtoday.com/yp/configuration_management.html

If you go to only one place for the most comprehensive set of links on the topic of software configuration management, this is the place to go. It has *everything* (or at least it always seems to) and is updated regularly. It used to be maintained by Andre van der Hoek but has since been passed on to the folks who host the *CM Today* newsletter and cmtalk mailing list.

## CM CROSSROADS—ONLINE COMMUNITY AND RESOURCE CENTER FOR CM PROFESSIONALS

- http://www.cmcrossroads.com/

If you go to only two places for the most comprehensive set of links on the topic of software configuration management, this is the second place to go. It hasn't been around as long as the CM Yellow Pages, but it is very comprehensive, has a regular newsletter, and has a growing list of resource links on several topics related to SCM.

## CM TODAY—DAILY CONFIGURATION MANAGEMENT NEWS

• http://www.cmtoday.com/

This configuration management (CM) newsletter and resource site is updated daily. The same site houses the CM Yellow Pages and CM job listings. It also has a Web page where you can subscribe to the cmtalk mailing list and view the message archives of the mailing list.

## UCM CENTRAL—UNIFIED CONFIGURATION MANAGEMENT

• http://www.ucmcentral.com

This is another good site with resources and a portal and links to information about various tools and vendors. It also contains several informative articles, diagrams, and templates.

## ACME—ASSEMBLING CONFIGURATION MANAGEMENT ENVIRONMENTS (FOR SOFTWARE)

• http://acme.bradapp.net/

This is the Web site created by one of the authors of this book in his quest to uncover and disseminate SCM patterns and best practices. The site has an extensive list of SCM definitions, a set of SCM recommended readings, several papers and presentations by the authors about SCM patterns and best practices, and a respectable collection of links to SCM research and practice (unfortunately, the links need much updating).

## THE SOFTWARE ENGINEERING INSTITUTE'S SCM PUBLICATIONS

- http://www.sei.cmu.edu/legacy/scm/

This provides some links to general resources, FAQs, and, best of all, the SEI CM documents archive. Although they are somewhat dated, most of these papers are excellent, and many are considered "classics" in the field. Of particular note are the following papers by Susan Dart and Peter Feiler:

- "The Spectrum of Functionality in CM Systems," by Susan Dart
- "Concepts in CM," by Susan Dart
- "The Past, Present and Future of CM," by Susan Dart
- "Configuration Management Models in Commercial Environments," by Peter Feiler
- "Transaction-Oriented CM: A Case Study," by Peter Feiler and Grace Downey

## STEVE EASTERBROOK'S CONFIGURATION MANAGEMENT RESOURCE GUIDE

- http://www.cmiiug.com/sites.htm

This is a great resource for addresses, points of contact, and titles in a plain FAQ-like format. The parent site is also the home of the Institute for Configuration Management (http://www.icmhq.com/).

## THE SOFTWARE CONFIGURATION MANAGEMENT FAQ

- http://www.daveeaton.com/scm/CMFAQ.html

This site is a classic, compiled and maintained by Dave Eaton, who put together the first such FAQ for the comp.software.config-mgmt Usenet newsgroup. The

FAQ consists of three separate FAQs: One is on SCM in general, one is on version control and SCM tools, and another is on problem-tracking tools.

## THE ASSOCIATION FOR CONFIGURATION AND DATA MANAGEMENT

- http://www.acdm.org/

## SOFTWARE ENGINEERING RESOURCE LIST FOR SOFTWARE CONFIGURATION MANAGEMENT

- http://wwwsel.iit.nrc.ca/favs/CMfavs.html

This is a very nice SCM site from the Software Engineering Group (SEG) at the Institute for Information Technology.

## R. S. PRESSMAN AND ASSOCIATES SOFTWARE ENGINEERING RESOURCES FOR SCM

- http://www.rspa.com/spi/SCM.html

This is Roger Pressman's site of SCM links for software engineering (Pressman is the author of several well-known software engineering books).

## SEWEB SOFTWARE CONFIGURATION MANAGEMENT RESOURCES AT FLINDERS UNIVERSITY

- http://see.cs.flinders.edu.au/seweb/scm/

## PASCAL MOLLI'S "CM BUBBLES" SCM RESOURCES PAGE

- http://www.loria.fr/~molli/cm-index.html

## THE USENET NEWSGROUP COMP.SOFTWARE.CONFIG-MGMT

- news:comp.software.config-mgmt

This newsgroup can now also be read, searched, and posted to using Google: http://groups.google.com/groups?hl=en&lr=&group=comp.software. config-mgmt

Appendix B

# Tool Support for SCM Patterns

*with Bob Ventimiglia[1]*

This appendix describes how the SCM patterns in this book map to the concepts implemented by several commonly used software version control (VC) tools (see Table B-1). The intent is not to give the operational details for a

### Table B-1. Some Commonly Used Version Control Tools

| Tool | Vendor | Web Site |
|------|--------|----------|
| VSS—Visual Source Safe | Microsoft | http://msdn.microsoft.com/ssafe/ |
| CVS—the Concurrent Versions System | CVS is open source; development is hosted by Collab.Net | http://www.cvshome.org/ |
| Perforce | Perforce Software | http://www.perforce.com/ |
| BitKeeper | BitMover Inc. | http://www.bitkeeper.com/ |
| AccuRev | AccuRev Inc. | http://www.accurev.com/ |

---

1. Bob Ventimiglia is a consultant with Merant. He can be found at http://www.bobev.com.

**Table B–1. Some Commonly Used Version Control Tools** *continued*

| Tool | Vendor | Web Site |
|------|--------|----------|
| ClearCase | Rational Software | http://www.rational.com/products/clearcase/ |
| UCM—Unified Change Management | Rational Software | http://www.rational.com/products/clearcase/ |
| CM Synergy | Telelogic | http://www.telelogic.com/products/synergy/ |
| StarTeam | Starbase | http://www.starbase.com/products/starteam/ |
| PVCS Dimensions | Merant PVCS | http://www.merant.com/pvcs |
| PVCS Version Manager | Merant PVCS | http://www.merant.com/pvcs |
| MKSource Integrity | MKS Inc. | http://www.mks.com/products/sie/ |

"cookbook" or "how-to" but to refer to the tool-specific mechanisms and how they work together to support our SCM patterns. This should provide a conceptual base for looking up detailed usage instructions in the product documentation.

Table B-1 shows the product name and vendor information for the list of tools that will be discussed. For each tool, we briefly describe its basic concepts and terminology to provide a high-level overview of how to use it to perform the following common activities:

- Create a *Private Workspace (6)*

- Configure and populate it from a *Repository (7)* or from a codeline

- Create a change task and/or a *Task Branch (19)*

- Update the workspace with the latest state of the codeline

- Perform a *Task Level Commit (11)* of the changes from the workspace into the codeline

- Create a new codeline (for a *Mainline (4)*, an *Active Development Line (5)*, a *Release Line (17)*, a *Release-Prep Code Line (18)*, or a *Third Party Codeline (10)*)

- Create a label or version identifier for one of the *Named Stable Bases (20)*

Table B-2 through Table B-13 summarize this mapping of tool concepts to pattern concepts for each of the tools in this appendix.

## VSS—VISUAL SOURCE SAFE

VSS is one of the more commonly used VC tools among those using a Microsoft-based integrated development environment (IDE) such as Visual C++. Although it has a nice GUI and very seamless integration with the programming language environment, VSS is among the less capable tools described here. VSS has relatively limited support for branching and parallel development. It is not intended for projects that regularly require multiple codelines.

### Table B-2. Mapping of SCM Pattern Concepts to VSS Concepts

| SCM Pattern Concept Name | VSS Concept Name | Comments |
|---|---|---|
| Repository | Master project | |
| Development Workspace | Working directory | |
| Codeline | Share and branch | See also *pin* |
| Change Task | N/A | |
| Workspace Update | Get project | From the master/codeline project into the working directory |
| Task-Level Commit | Check-in project | |
| Task Branch | N/A | |
| Label | Label project | |

A repository in VSS corresponds to a database that holds one or more *master projects*. VSS supports "project-oriented" operations that operate on all selected files or all the files defined to be in a specified project. A master project is simply a VSS project that holds the master copies of a set of files and their latest versions (it also serves as the mainline).

A development workspace is created in VSS by associating a project with a *working directory*.

The working directory is populated by performing a project-oriented *get* operation to retrieve the latest versions of a project's files into the working directory for read-only access. A *checkout* operation is used to copy a writable copy of a file into the working directory.

The working directory may be updated with the latest project versions by doing another *get* project operation from the master (or codeline) project into the working directory.

Changes from the working directory may be "committed" to the codeline by doing a *checkin* project operation from the working directory into the master (or codeline) project where the latest versions of the project are stored for that codeline.

VSS doesn't have a separate notion of a change task; it relies on project operations in the working directory to be performed in task order. And because branching in VSS is limited, branches are almost never created for the purpose of a single task.

A new codeline is created for a project by *sharing and branching* the files in that project to create a new copy of that project.

- The *share* operation (formerly called *pin*) links and copies the selected file versions from the master project into a new project for the new codeline.

- The *branch* operation makes sure the selected files are copies (rather than links) and may have their contents revised and evolved independently of the project from which they were initially shared.

A new label is created by performing the *label* operation on the selected set of files in the project.

The following are caveats for using VSS:

- The *get* operation works properly for a workspace update only when you check out the files you want to change *before* making your local changes to them. If you modify your local copies but don't invoke the *get* operation until just before you are ready to check them in, VSS won't know that your locally modified files were checked out before other versions that were checked in after you made your changes (but before you checked the files out). If you make sure to check out the files before you make changes to your local copies, VSS will know to perform the *merge* operation for any files that you changed that also changed in the codeline

- VSS doesn't effectively support a branching depth of more than two levels. If you do this, VSS won't remember the full merge ancestry more than one level deep, and merging and reconciling changes more than one level back will be more difficult.

## CVS—THE CONCURRENT VERSIONS SYSTEM

CVS is open source software and is probably one of the most widely known and used version control tools in common use today. CVS supports most of these pattern concepts using the following *copy-modify-merge* model.

- *Copy*—A developer sets up a working directory and requests a working copy of the files in the project by checking out files from the project into the working directory. The syntax would be "checkout *<options> <module-name>*" (or "update *<options> <codeline-name>*" to populate the workspace with the latest files from the codeline).

- *Modify*—The developer edits any working copies of files in the working directory, using the "checkout" command.

- *Merge*—The developer performs a "commit" operation to check in the modifications to the repository

The main commands used are *tag, checkout, update,* and *commit.* One typically uses the "-R" option with the *update, commit,* and *tag* commands to apply recursively to all files in the working directory. Branches for a codeline or a task

## Table B-3. Mapping of SCM Pattern Concepts to CVS Concepts

| SCM Pattern Concept Name | CVS Concept Name | Comments |
|---|---|---|
| Repository | Repository | Also known as CVSROOT |
| Development Workspace | *Working directory* or *working copies* | Create using *cvs checkout -R . . .* or *cvs update -R . . .* ; also see *cvs export* |
| Codeline | Branch | Create using *cvs tag -b* |
| Change Task | N/A | |
| Workspace Update | Update | *cvs update* |
| Task-Level Commit | Commit | *cvs commit* |
| Task Branch | Branch | Create using *cvs tag -b* |
| Label | Tag | See also *rtag* |
| Third Party Codeline | Vendor branch | Use *cvs import -b* |

branch are created using the *tag* command with the "-b" option. The *update* command synchronizes the developer's workspace with the latest state of the named codeline. When the time comes to create a label (or, if desired, a checkpoint), the *tag* command can again be used (this time without the "-b" option).

As a special case, CVS was specifically designed to support the concept of a *vendor branch* (a *Third Party Codeline (10)*). The *import* command was tailor made for this purpose.

The following are some caveats for using CVS:

- CVS doesn't have GUI support for branching and merging as nice as that of many of the commercial tools (but other open source GUIs exist and more seem to be written every year). This places the burden on you to draw mentally the visual picture of the codeline and branching structure in your mind.

- CVS also isn't quite as expert at tracking merge history as some of the more advanced commercial tools. If a version has been merged and a particular set of changes within the file were intentionally left unchanged (or changed differently), subsequent merges will continue to present those same changes, even though the version they came from already had its differences "reconciled." Merge technology in many of the more capable version control tools knows not to look at the contents of changes for versions that are already part of the "merge ancestry" of the current version.

## PERFORCE

Perforce is a very commonly used, simple but powerful commercial VC tool with outstanding support for branching and merging. It bills itself as the "fast software configuration management system" and prides itself on performance and distributed TCP/IP client-server operation.

A repository in Perforce is called a *depot*. The Perforce server centrally manages access to the depot from connecting clients.

A Perforce workspace is called a *client workspace* and is configured by specifying a *client spec* to create a *client view* in the workspace. A codeline is called a *branch* in Perforce (as is a task branch). Perforce tracks the changes between parent and child branches, so it knows when a file version has already been merged and reconciled or not.

### Table B-4. Mapping of SCM Pattern Concepts to Perforce Concepts

| SCM Pattern Concept Name | Perforce Concept Name | Comments |
| --- | --- | --- |
| Repository | Depot | |
| Development Workspace | Client workspace and client spec | *p4 client* and *p4 sync* |
| Codeline | Branch | *p4 branch* and *p4 integrate* |
| Change Task | Changelist | Also see jobs |
| Workspace Update | Sync | *p4 sync* and *p4 resolve* |
| Task-Level Commit | Submit | *p4 submit* |
| Task Branch | Branch | *p4 branch* and *p4 integrate -b* |
| Label | Label | *p4 label* and *p4 labelsync* |

Perforce uses an *atomic change transaction* model, where an operation either succeeds on all files involved in the operation or on none of them (an unexpected interrupt should never create a partially completed update or commit). Perforce's branches (and resulting branch tree) are depotwide rather than file-specific. This makes for a conceptually powerful branching model for managing parallel development with multiple codelines. (Other VC tools achieve this result with "projects" or "workspaces" or "streams" using a hierarchical structure.) Perforce also has a means of allowing configurable change-review notifications, daemons, and triggers to add customized checks and verification where desired.

A Perforce workspace is set up by appropriately setting the P4PORT and P4CLIENT environment variables and running *p4 client* to edit the client spec to the desired client view.

Once the workspace is set up and configured, *p4 sync* will populate the workspace with read-only copies of the latest files selected by the client spec. Changes are made by using the *p4 edit* command to obtain a writable copy of a file to modify.

The *p4 sync* command is also used to update a workspace. Checked-out files will not be modified by *p4 sync*. A *p4 resolve* command must be used to reconcile the differences between the checked-out files and the latest versions in the codeline.

Files revised with the *edit, add,* and *delete* commands are added to a *changelist* that Perforce maintains for your workspace. Those changes can be committed to the depot using the *p4 submit* command. If any of your files aren't the most recent version on the codeline, you will get a submit error. Submit errors and merge conflicts are resolved using the *p4 resolve* command. You can use *p4 resolve -n* to see which files need to be resolved.

Branches are created using *p4 integrate.* The *integrate* command can also be used with a *branch spec* to make the branch name automatically remember the mappings for the branched files. (This is convenient to use for codelines and task branches when you have planned for them in advance.)

The *p4 label* command creates labels for releases, builds, and checkpoints. The *p4 labelsync* command can revise the set of files belonging to a label.

## BITKEEPER

BitKeeper bills itself as the "distributed" scalable SCM system. It also exhibits excellent performance and reliability. Rather than using a client-server model, BitKeeper uses a *fully replicated peer-to-peer model* of operation that enables fully disconnected use from the *master* repository. BitKeeper provides triggers that enable customization of the most common repository-wide and file-specific operations.

The key to understanding BitKeeper's operational model is to understand that every BitKeeper workspace is also a repository. Changes, in the form of change-sets, are made in a workspace, and developers can propagate change-sets back and forth between workspaces using *push* and *pull* operations. All change-set operations are atomic in BitKeeper.

Because of this simple but powerful model of distributed workspaces as repositories for transmitting and receiving change-sets, both codelines

### Table B-5. Mapping of SCM Pattern Concepts to BitKeeper Concepts

| SCM Pattern Concept Name | BitKeeper Concept Name | Comments |
| --- | --- | --- |
| Repository | Master repository | |
| Development Workspace | Developer repository | Create with *bk clone* |
| Codeline | Integration repository | Also see Line of Development (LOD) |
| Change Task | Change-set | Use *bk citool* or *bk commit*; also see *bk revtool* |
| Workspace Update | Pull and resolve | Use *bk pull* and *bk resolve* |
| Task-Level Commit | Commit and push | Use *bk citool*, *bk commit*, and *bk push*; also see *bk ci* |
| Task Branch | Developer repository | Also see Line of Development |
| Label | Change-set, also a tag | Use *bk tag*; also see *bk commit -s* |
| Checkpoint | Change-set, also a tag | Or just use *bk unpull* to roll back to previous state after an unsuccessful *bk pull* |

and task branches can be represented as workspaces in BitKeeper. Bit-Keeper workspaces operate like an unnamed branch. With BitKeeper, you plan your codelines and create a hierarchy of integration workspaces for each codeline in your hierarchy. You don't have to create branches in addition to codelines: When a change-set is pulled from another repository, the receiving workspace knows at that time which files had concurrent changes and creates branches for only those files. (Think of it as "branch on demand.")

A codeline corresponds to an integration repository used for pulling in change-sets and then pushing them to higher-level codelines in the hierarchy. A task branch corresponds to a development repository for a single development task, enabling private local changes to be made that won't be seen by other repositories until they choose to pull them in.

So developers don't need to keep track of both a task branch and a workspace. They just work in their workspace, and after their changes are done, BitKeeper takes care of worrying whether any files need to be branched. This eliminates the need in a lot of other VC tools to have merges between branches that don't change the file contents. This, combined with Bit-Keeper's merging technology, makes it very easy in BitKeeper to find the change-set that first introduced a particular line of code that was propagated across several codelines.

Another important aspect of BitKeeper is that a change-set is repository wide: It captures not only all the changes but the context of the changes as well (the state of the repository in which the changes were made). This lets a change set also act as a label or a checkpoint. It also means BitKeeper is "time-safe" in its ability to track the historical evolution of change-sets as they are pushed and pulled throughout a "promotion hierarchy" of workspaces.

Like most of the other tools described here, BitKeeper may be used via a GUI or from the command line. The typical developer scenario for making a change follows.

1.  Create a new workspace using *bk clone* from the parent repository (or use an existing workspace without any pending changes). One can use the *bk get* or *bk edit* operations to populate and access files in the repository to make changes (*get* obtains read-only copies of files, whereas *edit* obtains writable copies).

2.  Use *bk pull* to update your workspace with the latest changes from the parent repository (the codeline). Use *bk resolve* immediately afterward to merge and resolve any resulting conflicts from the *pull* operation.

3.  When changes are complete, the *bk citool* operation checks them in to your local repository. The *bk commit* operation then creates a change-set for your changes. The *bk push* operation then propagates the changes back to the parent repository.

4.  Create labels using *bk tag* or with the "-s" option to the *commit* operation.

## ACCUREV

AccuRev is a more recent VC tool offering that is not as well known as most of the other tools described here. Like Perforce, AccuRev uses the term "depot" to refer to a repository. Also like Perforce, AccuRev prides itself on performance, distributed TCP/IP client-server operation, and atomic change transactions (as well as integrated issue tracking).

### Table B-6. Mapping of SCM Pattern Concepts to AccuRev Concepts

| SCM Pattern Concept Name | AccuRev Concept Name | Comments |
| --- | --- | --- |
| Repository | Depot | |
| Development Workspace | Workspace | *accurev mkws* and *accurev mksnap* |
| Codeline | Stream | Also see backing stream and base stream |
| Change Task | Transaction | Also see workspace stream |
| Workspace Update | Update | See also the *pop* command and *merge -o* |
| Task-Level Commit | Promote | *promote -k* moves changes from the workspace stream so they are visible in the codeline |
| Task Branch | Workspace stream | Also see dynamic stream |
| Label | Real version | See also virtual versions and snapshot streams |
| Checkpoint | Checkpoint | Create using the *keep* command |

One of AccuRev's distinguishing features is that it is *time safe*: It doesn't just version all your data, it also versions all your metadata. So in addition to being able to track and reproduce prior contents of files, it can also track and reproduce prior definitions of labels (which it calls checkpoints and streams) as well as other AccuRev metadata.

Central to understanding AccuRev is its simple but powerful notion of a *stream*. AccuRev streams can be used as codelines, workspaces, and labels. An AccuRev stream is a logical set of files and file versions in the depot. An AccuRev workspace is simply a place in which you perform work on a stream.

Streams may be static or dynamic. Static streams may not have their contents changed and may serve as known stable configurations or even fill the same purpose as a label. Dynamic streams can have their contents changed in a workspace.

Dynamic streams may be linked together hierarchically to create a promotion hierarchy for workflow and integration. The topmost stream in the hierarchy is called the *base stream* and serves as a mainline. Other parent streams serve as a *backing stream* to their child streams and provide a starting point from the mainline for other development projects (codelines) that will be long-lived. The child streams are *workspace streams* where developers make their changes to the codeline.

So in AccuRev, a base stream acts as a mainline, a backing stream acts as a codeline, and a workspace stream acts as both a change task and a task branch (with the changes in the stream associated with a transaction). A *static stream* is a snapshot that may serve as a label.

AccuRev also has *real versions* and *virtual versions*. A real version is created anytime a stream is checkpointed using the *keep* command. A virtual version is an alias for a real version but allows the name of the virtual version to be used as the corresponding real version evolves dynamically over time. So the history of a virtual version is a progression of real version names and their sequential numbers.

AccuRev may be used via a GUI or from the command line. The typical developer scenario for making a change follows.

1.   Create your workspace using the *accurev mkws* command. Then edit files at will in your workspace stream.

2. To update your workspace, do an *accurev update* followed by an *accurev merge -o* to resolve any resulting conflicts.

3. To commit your changes, do an *accurev keep -m* to create a checkpoint of your stream, and then do an *accurev promote -k* to commit your changes from the workspace stream to its backing stream.

## CLEARCASE—BASE FUNCTIONALITY (NON-UCM)

ClearCase is among the more popular and more sophisticated version control tools on the market. Like Perforce, ClearCase has very conceptually powerful parallel development and branching capabilities. ClearCase has a *base* option, which lets you roll your own process and policies based on the framework it provides, as well as a UCM option, which supports Rational's Unified Change Management for activity-based SCM using higher-level concepts than base ClearCase alone.

---

### Table B-7. Mapping of SCM Pattern Concepts to Base ClearCase Concepts

| *SCM Pattern Concept Name* | *Base ClearCase Concept Name* | *Comments* |
| --- | --- | --- |
| Repository | Versioned Object Base (VOB) | |
| Development Workspace | View and config spec, also view profile | *cleartool mkview,* cleartool *edcs,* make branch with view profile |
| Codeline | Project branch | *cleartool mkbrtype, mkbranch* config spec rules, view profiles |
| Change Task | N/A | |
| Workspace Update | *findmerge* | *cleartool findmerge,* MergeManager |
| Task-Level Commit | *findmerge* | *cleartool findmerge,* MergeManager |
| Task Branch | Private branch | *cleartool mkbrtype,* make private branch |
| Label | Label | *cleartool mklbtype, cleartool* mklabel |

ClearCase is one of the most configurable tools on the market, providing customizable triggers for just about every operation imaginable. One thing ClearCase does that most other VC tools do not is to version its directories as well as files. That means it remembers which files participated in which version of a particular directory.

The base ClearCase option does not directly support the notion of a change task, although task branches are commonly used for this purpose. The Clear-Case GUI on Windows platforms supports *private branches* and *view profiles*, which are ways of automating support for task branches and creating workspaces with the proper configuration of versions from the project branch. Using private branches, you follow this typical development scenario.

1.  Create a view, using an appropriate view profile for the desired project. This will also ask whether a private branch should be used.

2.  Perform checkouts in the view (and check-ins if using a task branch) to make the necessary changes.

3.  "Finish" the private branch by merging the changes back into the codeline.

From the command line, without private branches, this is the typical scenario.

1.  Create a view using the *mkview* command.

2.  Create a branch (if desired) using the *mkbrtype* command.

3.  Configure the view to select the appropriate versions using *edcs* or *setcs*.

**Note:** The previous three steps are typically automated and simplified into a single script or batch file that takes a task name (to use as part of the name for the view and the branch) and some kind of project identifier to determine the view configuration. The details of where the view's file storage is created and which specific configuration rules to use are often encapsulated into this script so that the typical developer doesn't have to worry about those details.

Perform checkouts and (if using a task branch) checkins as desired. If you are working on a task branch, any checkins are effectively private versions that are captured in the VOB for posterity but appear only on your private branch and not in the codeline.

When you desire, update the view using the *findmerge* command (typically with the *-flatest* or *-fversion* option). This is not necessary if your view is a *dynamic view* selecting the */LATEST* versions of the codeline. ClearCase's virtual file system ensures that the versions in a dynamic view are always synchronized with the */LATEST* versions specified by the view's config spec. Snapshot views and views that select a labeled state of the codeline (rather than */LATEST*) will need to be updated before you do a commit.

Commit changes by going into an integration view and doing a *findmerge* *-ftag* (or *-fversion*) of the changes from your development task/view into the integration view (here again, a script or a batch file is often used to simplify the interface and conceptual complexity of the *findmerge* command).

Labels are created using the *mklbtype* command to create the label name and using the *mklabel* command to apply the label to selected versions. A checkpoint maybe created by applying a label to the entire view or just to the latest versions on the task branch, or even by just recording a timestamp for the most recent checkpoint.

## CLEARCASE—UNIFIED CHANGE MANAGEMENT (UCM)

The UCM option for ClearCase adds higher-level concepts and provides direct support for change tasks and update and commit operations (to a much greater degree than view profiles and private branches). A codeline may be regarded as a UCM *project* to which developers may subscribe. Each project may have an integration stream (where changes are merged into the codeline) and one or more development streams. A UCM stream is at once both a workspace and a task branch of sorts. UCM also directly supports the notion of an *activity* and allows a stream to encompass more than one activity (so it need not be limited to a single task). UCM directly supports each of the SCM pattern concepts as follows.

Start a new change task by creating a new development stream for an associated project (or using an existing development stream). Then create a new

## Table B-8. Mapping of SCM Pattern Concepts to UCM ClearCase Concepts

| SCM Pattern Concept Name | UCM Concept Name | Comments |
| --- | --- | --- |
| Repository | Versioned Object Base (VOB) | |
| Development Workspace | Development stream | *cleartool mkstream* |
| Codeline | Project | *cleartool mkproject* plus an integration stream and foundation baseline |
| Change Task | Activity | *cleartool mkactivity* |
| Workspace Update | *rebase* | *cleartool* Rebase |
| Task-Level Commit | Deliver | *cleartool deliver* |
| Task Branch | Activity | An activity in a development stream |
| Label | Baseline | *cleartool mkbl* |
| Codeline Policy | Project policy settings | |
| Integration Workspace | Integration stream | |

activity to work on in that development stream as the current activity. UCM will capture the versions associated with that activity as its change-set.

Updating one's workspace corresponds to performing a *rebase* operation for the current activity in a development stream. Committing the changes corresponds to a *deliver* operation.

A UCM project can be configured with certain codeline policy elements, such as requiring a *rebase* before delivery.

UCM *baselines* correspond to labels and may be full or partial/incremental. Baselines may have a promotion level associated with them to indicate the level of verification and quality assurance they have undergone (for example, initial, rejected, built, tested, released). Each baseline must be associated with a UCM *component* (which is a source tree of files in a VOB).

## CM SYNERGY

CM Synergy was once known as Continuus and is a very powerful process-centered SCM tool that uses tasks, projects, and folders along with highly configurable workflow.

CM Synergy uses the terms "repository" and "database" interchangeably. A CM Synergy database holds one or more projects or products. All the files for a particular system are usually mapped to a top-level project.

Workspaces in CM Synergy are called *work areas* or *working projects*. A working project is created simply by checking out the entire project into the designated work area. The work area provides a file-system-based view of a project in terms of a component source tree of files and directories.

The logical unit of change in CM Synergy is a *task*. CM Synergy has no need to create a new branch for a task. Developers simply set up their workspace and work on their assigned task(s) in that workspace. An *update members* (or *reconfigure*) operation is used to update the work area's working project. In this manner, a *project object* corresponds to a codeline.

### Table B-9. Mapping of SCM Pattern Concepts to CM Synergy Concepts

| *SCM Pattern Concept Name* | *CM Synergy Concept Name* | *Comments* |
|---|---|---|
| Repository | Project | Also *see base model* |
| Development Workspace | Work area | Also see *working project* |
| Codeline | Project object | |
| Change Task | Task | |
| Workspace Update | Update members | Also *see reconfigure* |
| Task-Level Commit | Complete task | Also called *check-in task* |
| Task Branch | Task | |
| Label | Baseline | |
| Codeline Policy | Project template | |

When changes for a task are finished, a *complete task* (or *check in task*) operation commits the changes to the project for other developers to see.

CM Synergy also supports the notion of a *release stream*, which is a more formal sort of codeline corresponding to the *Release Line* pattern. To create a label in CM Synergy, one does a *release* (check-in) of an entire project. This captures the current configuration of a project and associates a release name with it by automatically setting the release attribute on all object members of the project.

## STARTEAM

StarTeam, a relative newcomer on the process-oriented SCM tool scene is becoming more well known and bills itself as an easy-to-use tool with a configurable workflow that can read and work with VSS and PVCS Version Manger (VM) repositories. StarTeam uses a centralized, SQL-compliant database as its repository. Windows, UNIX, and Web clients access *projects* containing *folder/file hierarchies* managed by the repository. A *StarTeam view* is a set of *working folders* and *working files* in a project representing both workspaces and codelines. All development activities take place in a StarTeam view.

A distinguishing feature of StarTeam is its ability to combine—in a single tab-based view—definition and linking of files, changes, requirements, tasks, and topics. So in addition to tracking and reproducing changes to files, it can track and electronically link files with changes, tasks, and topics, and with each other. StarTeam *topics* allow Usenet-style threaded conversations to occur between team members; the topic can be linked to tasks and other StarTeam objects.

*Changes* and *tasks* are the logical units of change in StarTeam and, although it is possible, there is no need to create a new branch for a change or a task. StarTeam *process rules* achieve the same goal. Process rules ensure that all file revisions created are also linked and pinned to a change or a task. Developers need only to follow the link to check out and work on their assigned files.

The workspace or StarTeam view is updated by checking in or merging files that have been modified. Tasks are completed by updating them. And finally, a new view label is created from the updated view and completed tasks.

## Table B-10. Mapping of SCM Pattern Concepts to StarTeam Concepts

| SCM Pattern Concept Name | CM Synergy Concept Name | Comments |
|---|---|---|
| Repository | Repository | Also see *project* |
| Development Workspace | Working files/folders | Also see *view* |
| Codeline | Project view | Also see *reference view* and *branching view* |
| Change Task | Task | |
| Workspace Update | Check-in | Also see *update status* and *view compare/merge* |
| Task-Level Commit | Merge | |
| Task Branch | Branching view | Also see *process rules*, *project view*, and *reference view* |
| Label | Label | See also *view label* and *revision label* |
| Checkpoint | View label | |

A new mainline is created using the File/Project/New dialog. An initial baseline workspace is created using the Folder/New dialog, which relates the StarTeam folder hierarchy to the user's operating system directory structure.

A new task is created by selecting the Task Tab and then the Tasks/New Task dialog. The Link tool is used to associate files to the task. The linked files are edited using the File/Edit dialog or using the operating system editor.

The workspace is updated using the File/Check-in dialog, which updates the workspace and the codeline.

A revision label identifying all the files in the view is created using the View/Labels dialog and selecting *revision* as the label type.

The task is then updated by selecting the task and the RMB/Update dialog.

## PVCS DIMENSIONS

PVCS Dimensions gained its fame under the name PCMS from SQL Software. It has undergone several new versions since being acquired by Merant and incorporated into the PVCS product line. It is a very complete SCM tool that covers not only version management but also change management and process management.

PVCS Dimensions supports the concept of both *products* and *projects*. A product typically maps to a top-level project in the database.

A workspace in PVCS corresponds to a *workset*. Developers can share a common workset or may be allowed to create a private workset to hold their changes.

Change tasks are called *work packages* and may also be made to correspond to what Dimensions refers to as a *change document* using Dimensions's object relationships and linking capabilities.

### Table B-11. Mapping of SCM Pattern Concepts to PVCS Dimensions Concepts

| *SCM Pattern Concept Name* | *PVCS Dimensions Concept Name* | *Comments* |
|---|---|---|
| Repository | Base database | Typically a product or project within a base database, depending on the repository level |
| Development Workspace | Private workset | |
| Codeline | Named branch | Also could be a workset |
| Change Task | Work package | See also change document |
| Workspace Update | N/A | Updates the workset with the latest versions from the codeline (also see check-in) |
| Task-Level Commit | Promote action | Promotes a change task from an implementation status to a verification status |
| Task Branch | Work package | See also change document and named branch |
| Label | Baseline | Also see create revised baseline and certain kinds of named branches |
| Codeline Policy | Control plan | Captures team development process and rules |

Changes are committed by *promoting* the changes in a workset from an implementation state to a verification state.

Codelines are created by making a named branch or by using an integration workset into which other worksets are merged for the codeline.

Labels correspond to *baselines* that may be created for a product.

## PVCS VERSION MANAGER

PVCS VM has been around a long time and, as a result, is one of the more commonly used commercial VC tools. It is well known for its *promotion modeling* capability, which allows customers to define team development tasks, worksets, projects, and their progression from initial development of changes to increasing promotion levels of stability and quality assurance.

A PVCS *project database* can hold one or more *projects*, each of which can have its own project configuration options. A *promotion model* is a set of *promotion groups*, where each promotion group defines a level or milestone in a particular development cycle.

**Table B-12. Mapping of SCM Pattern Concepts to PVCS Version Manager Concepts**

| SCM Pattern Concept Name | PVCS VM Concept Name | Comments |
|---|---|---|
| Repository | Project database | Also see project root |
| Development Workspace | Workspace | Also see subproject and workfile location |
| Codeline | Branch | |
| Change Task | N/A | |
| Workspace Update | N/A | |
| Task-Level Commit | Check-in | |
| Task Branch | N/A | |
| Label | Version label | Also see baselining |
| Codeline Policy | Promotion groups | Also see project configuration options |

A developer typically creates a workspace by opening a project database and selecting a project to view in the workspace, specifying the *workfile location* from which files will be checked in and out.

The workspace is populated by getting unlocked versions of the files (*get*) in the project view. A file may be edited by performing a checkout to create a writable copy. This locks the file against checkout by other developers in the project.

Typical PVCS operation doesn't encourage parallel development for individual projects and their codelines (so there is no direct equivalent of a workspace update that reconciles changes without doing a check-in), but *variant projects* and *subprojects* may be used to create branches that correspond to alternate codelines of development.

The *checkin* operation is the way changes are committed to the project.

*Version labels* may be created for a project to represent version identifier labels.

## MKS INTEGRITY (ENTERPRISE EDITION)

Source Integrity (SI) is very similar in its operation to PVCS Version Manager. SI *projects* are sets of files that are grouped together as a single body or scope of work. Projects may be broken down into subprojects. Project *members* are source files. A workspace is called a *sandbox* in SI. Codelines and task branches are called *development paths*, and version identifiers are called *project checkpoints* and may be assigned project *labels*.

One of SI's most powerful features is *change packages*, which can be used to hold a single change task or a collection of changes to move back and forth between a master project and a development path for a variant project (and vice versa).

A sandbox is created and associated with a project and the latest versions of its members. Files are checked out in the sandbox as needed. Checkouts lock the file in the project as with PVCS VM.

The sandbox may be updated via a *resync* command, and all the changes made in the sandbox may be grouped into a change package, if desired.

Eventually, a *checkin* command commits the changes to the project.

Codelines are created by making a variant project of a master project and associating it with a development path.

## Table B-13. Mapping of SCM Pattern Concepts to MKS Source Integrity Concepts

| SCM Pattern Concept Name | MKS Integrity Concept Name | Comments |
| --- | --- | --- |
| Repository | Top-level project | |
| Development Workspace | Sandbox | |
| Codeline | Development path | Also see projects and subproject |
| Change Task | Change package | |
| Workspace Update | Resync | |
| Task-Level Commit | Check-in | |
| Task Branch | Change package | |
| Label | Project checkpoint | Also labels |

Checkpointing a project creates a new version identifier for the last state of the project. Labels may be created explicitly and associated with a checkpoint or with the current versions in a project.

## FURTHER READING

See the vendor home pages mentioned earlier for the definitive sources of information on all these tools. Also see the following.

- The book *Essential SourceSafe*, by Ted Roche and Larry C. Whipple (Roche and Whipple 2001), is a basic guide for VSS installation, administration, and usage.

- See the VSS technical FAQ and resources at http://msdn.microsoft.com/ssafe/technical/ (and an unofficial FAQ at http://www.michaelis.net/SourceSafe/Faq.htm).

- *Open Source Development with CVS* (Fogel and Bar 2001) is an excellent guide to using CVS.

- *Subversion* is intended to be the next generation open source replacement for CVS. Its home page is currently at http://subversion.tigris.org/.

- *Practical Software Configuration Management* (Mikkelsen and Pherigo 1997) also covers some aspects of CVS usage but is not as recent as Fogel's book.

- Pascal Molli maintains an excellent collection of CVS-related links and information at http://www.loria.fr/~molli/cvs-index.html.

- Brian White's *Software Configuration Management Strategies and Rational ClearCase* (White 2000) provides an overview of UCM.

- Christian Goetze maintains an "unofficial" ClearCase FAQ at http://www.cg-soft.com/faq/clearcase.html.

- Damon Poole's paper "The TimeSafe Property—A Formal Statement of Immutability in CM" can be found at http://www.accurev.com/accurev/info/timesafe.html.

- Alexis Leon's *Guide to Software Configuration Management* (Leon 2000) has an overview of several dozen SCM tools in its appendixes.

- Susan Dart's *Configuration Management: The Missing Link in Web Engineering* (Dart 2000) contains a great deal of information, including several sections on evaluating and selecting CM tools for the enterprise.

# Photo Credits

Page 3    Photo by Russell Lee, May 1938. Library of Congress, Prints &
          Photographs Division, FSA-OWI Collection, Reproduction Num-
          ber: LC-USF33-011474-M3 DLC.

Page 19   Photo by Arthur Rothstein. Library of Congress, Prints & Photo-
          graphs Division, FSA-OWI Collection, Reproduction Number:
          LC-USF34-024346-D.

Page 33   Photo by Russell Lee, May 1938. Library of Congress, Prints &
          Photographs Division, FSA-OWI Collection, Reproduction Num-
          ber: LC-USF33-011692-M4.

Page 49   Photo by John Vachon. Library of Congress, Prints & Photo-
          graphs Division, FSA-OWI Collection, Reproduction Number:
          LC-USF34-064602-D DLC.

Page 59   Library of Congress, Prints & Photographs Division, Detroit Pub-
          lishing Company Collection. Reproduction Number: LC-D418-
          31625 DLC.

Page 67   Photo by David Meyers. Library of Congress, Prints & Photo-
          graphs Division, FSA-OWI Collection, Reproduction Number:
          LC-USF33-015598-M2.

Page 79   Photo by Russell Lee. Library of Congress, Prints & Photographs
          Division, FSA-OWI Collection, Reproduction Number: LC-USF33-
          013141-M1.

Page 87   Reprinted with permission of the Everett Collection.

Page 97    Photo by Alfred T. Palmer Library of Congress, Prints & Photographs Division, FSA-OWI Collection, Reproduction Number: LC-USW361-138.

Page 103   Photo by John Vachon. Library of Congress, Prints & Photographs Division, FSA-OWI Collection, Reproduction Number: LC-USF34-061836-D.

Page 111   Photo by Alfred T. Palmer. Library of Congress, Prints & Photographs Division, FSA-OWI Collection, Reproduction Number: LC-USE6-D-000162.

Page 117   Photo by John Collier. Library of Congress, Prints & Photographs Division, FSA-OWI Collection, Reproduction Number: LC-USF34-084002-C.

Page 123   Photo by Russell Lee. Library of Congress, Prints & Photographs Division, FSA-OWI Collection, Reproduction Number: LC-USF33-011632-M3.

Page 129   Photo by Alfred T. Palmer. Library of Congress, Prints & Photographs Division, FSA-OWI Collection, Reproduction Number: LC-USE6-D-005032.

Page 135   Photo by Alfred T. Palmer. Library of Congress, Prints & Photographs Division, FSA-OWI Collection, Reproduction Number: LC-USE6-D-007389.

Page 141   Photo by Marjory Collins. Library of Congress, Prints & Photographs Division, FSA-OWI Collection, Reproduction Number: LC-USW3-009019-D.

Page 147   Photo by Jack Delano. Library of Congress, Prints & Photographs Division, FSA-OWI Collection, Reproduction Number: LC-USW3-014014-E.

Page 153   Photo by Jack Delano. Library of Congress, Prints & Photographs Division, FSA-OWI Collection, Reproduction Number: LC-USW3-012717-D.

Page 157   Photo by John Collier. Library of Congress, Prints & Photographs Division, FSA-OWI Collection, Reproduction Number: LC-USW3-010723-C.

Page 163   Photo by Stephen P. Berczuk, © 2001.

# About the Photos

Chapter 1 (page 3): Barn erection. View of roofing operation from beneath, showing construction of the roof system. Southeast Missouri Farms Project.

Chapter 2 (page 19): Elevated structure and buildings. Lower Manhattan, New York, December 1941.

Chapter 3 (page 33): Patterns of tools painted on wall for easy identification. Lake Dick Project. Arkansas, September 1938.

Chapter 4 (page 49): On the main line. Bowdle, South Dakota, February 1942.

Chapter 5 (page 59): Construction, Grand Central Terminal. New York, between 1905 and 1915.

Chapter 6 (page 67): A government clerk's room, showing a desk with books, telephone and directory, and a desk lamp on it. Washington, D.C., 1939.

Chapter 7 (page 79): Cases of canned salmon in warehouse. Astoria, Oregon, September 1941.

Chapter 8 (page 87): with Charlie Chaplin.

Chapter 9 (page 97): Making wiring assemblies at a junction box on the fire wall for the right engine of a B-25 bomber, North American Aviation, Inc. Inglewood, California, July 1942.

Chapter 10 (page 103): Man who operates small grocery store and second-hand furniture store in his home. Chanute, Kansas, November 1940.

Chapter 11 (page 111): Proud of his job. Smiling worker in an eastern arsenal hand finishes the interior surface of a cradle for an 8-inch gun, railway carriage. 1942.

Chapter 12 (page 117): Louise Thompson, daughter of a newspaper editor in Richwood. She is a printer's devil. Richwood, West Virginia, September 1942.

Chapter 13 (page 123): Fighting fire of rice straw stack in rice field near Crowley, Louisiana. September 1938.

Chapter 14 (page 129): All the parts of an airplane engine, which has just undergone severe tests in a Midwest plant, are spread out for minute inspection. Continental Motors, Michigan, February 1942.

Chapter 15 (page 135): An experimental scale model of the B-25 plane is prepared for wind tunnel tests in the Inglewood, California, plant of North American Aviation, Inc. October 1942.

Chapter 16 (page 141): "Morgue" of the *New York Times* newspaper. Clippings on every conceivable subject are filed here for a reference. Editors and writers phone in for information. New York, September 1942.

Chapter 17 (page 147): Freight operations on the Chicago and Northwestern Railroad between Chicago and Clinton, Iowa. The rear brakeman signals the engineer to test the brakes by applying and releasing them. This is the signal for "apply." January 1943.

Chapter 18 (page 153): Train pulling out of a freight house at a Chicago and Northwestern Railroad yard. The wooden trestle is part of a long chain belt used to carry blocks of ice from the ice house to the freight house. Chicago, Illinois, December 1942.

Chapter 19 (page 157): Montour no. 4 mine of the Pittsburgh Coal Company. There are miles and miles of track in a mine, and the maintenance of the roadbed, ballast, and switches keeps a crew working constantly. Pittsburgh, Pennsylvania (vicinity), November 1942.

Chapter 20 (page 163): 1790's English-style barn, Union, Maine, October 2001.

# Bibliography

Adolph, Steve, Paul Bramble, Alistair Cockburn, and Andy Pols. 2003. *Patterns for Effective Use Cases*. Boston, Massachusetts: Addison-Wesley.

Alexander, C. 1979. *A Timeless Way of Building*. Oxford University Press.

Alexander, C., S. Ishikawa, and M. Silverstein. 1977. *A Pattern Language*. Oxford University Press.

Alexander, C., M. Silverstein, S. Angel, S. Ishikawa, and D. Abrams. 1975. *The Oregon Experiment*. Oxford University Press.

Allen, Thomas J. 1997a. "Architecture and Communication among Product Development Engineers." Cambridge, Massachusetts: M.I.T Sloan School. International Center for Research on Management Technology.

————. 1997b. "Organizational Structure for Product Development." Cambridge, Massachusetts: M.I.T. Sloan School. International Center for Research on Management Technology.

Allen, Thomas J., Breffni Tomlin, and Oscar Hauptman. 1998. "Combining Organizational and Physical Location to Manage Knowledge Dissemination." Cambridge, Massachusetts: M.I.T. Sloan School. International Center for Research on Management Technology.

Alpert, Sherman R., Kyle Brown, and Bobby Woolf. 1998. *The Design Patterns Smalltalk Companion*. The Software Patterns Series. Reading, Massachusetts: Addison-Wesley.

Appleton, Brad, Steve Berczuk, Ralph Cabrera, and Robert Orenstein. 1998. "Streamed Lines: Branching Patterns for Parallel Software Development." Paper read at Fifth Annual Conference on Pattern Languages of Programs, August 11–14, at Monticello, Illinois.

Babich, Wayne A. 1986. *Software Configuration Management: Coordination for Team Productivity*. Reading, Massachusetts: Addison-Wesley.

Bass, Len, Paul Clements, and Rick Kazman. 1998. *Software Architecture in Practice*. The SEI Series in Software Engineering. Reading, Massachusetts: Addison-Wesley.

Bays, Michael E. 1999. *Software Release Methodology*. Upper Saddle River, New Jersey: Prentice Hall PTR.

Beck, Kent. 2000. *Extreme Programming Explained: Embrace Change*. Boston: Addison-Wesley.

Berczuk, Stephen P. 1994. "Finding Solutions through Pattern Languages." *IEEE Computer* 27 (12):75–76.

Berczuk, Stephen P. 1995. "A Pattern for Separating Assembly and Processing." In *Pattern Languages of Program Design*, edited by J. Coplien and D. Schmidt. Reading, Massachusetts: Addison-Wesley.

————. 1996a. "Organizational Multiplexing: Patterns for Processing Satellite Telemetry with Distributed Teams." In *Pattern Languages of Program Design 2*, edited by J. Vlissides, J. Coplien, and N. Kerth. Reading, Massachusetts: Addison-Wesley.

Berczuk, Stephen P. 1996b. "Configuration Management Patterns." Paper read at Third Annual Conference on Pattern Languages of Programs, at Monticello, Illinois.

Berczuk, Stephen P., and Brad Appleton. 2000. "Getting Ready to Work: Patterns for a Developer's Workspace." Paper read at Pattern Languages of Programs, at Monticello, Illinois.

Berliner, Brian. 1990. *CVS II: Parallelizing Software Development*, USENIX Conference, Washington, D.C., January 26, 1990, pp. 341–352.

Booch, Grady. 1996. *Object Solutions: Managing the Object-Oriented Project*. Reading, Massachusetts: Addison-Wesley.

Booch, Grady, James Rumbaugh, and Ivar Jacobson. 1999. *The Unified Modeling Language User Guide*. The Addison-Wesley Object Technology Series. Reading, Massachusetts: Addison-Wesley.

Brooks, Frederick P. 1975. *The Mythical Man-Month*: *Essays on Software Engineering*. Reading, Massachusetts: Addison Wesley.

Brooks, Frederick P. 1995. *The Mythical Man-Month: Essays on Software Engineering, Anniversary Edition*. Reading, Massachusetts: Addison-Wesley.

Brown, William J., Hays W. McCormick, and Scott W. Thomas. 1999. *Antipatterns and Patterns in Software Configuration Management*. New York: Wiley.

Buschmann, Frank, Regine Meunier, Hans Rohnert, Peter Sommerlad, and Michael Stal. 1996. *Pattern-Oriented Software Architecture: A System of Patterns*. Chichester, England: Wiley.

Cabrera, Ralph, Brad Appleton, and Steve Berczuk. 1999. "Software Reconstruction: Patterns for Reproducing the Build." In *Proceedings of the Sixth Annual Conference on Pattern Languages of Program Design* at Monticello, Illinois.

Cockburn, Alistair. 2000. *Writing Effective Use Cases*. The Agile Series for Software Development. Boston: Addison-Wesley.

Conradi, Reidar, and Bernhard Westfechtel. 1998. "Version Control Models for Software Configuration Management." *ACM Computing Surveys* 30 (2): 232–278.

Coplien, James O. 1995. "A Generative Development Process Pattern Language." In *Pattern Languages of Program Design*. Reading, Massachusetts: Addison-Wesley.

Coplien, James O., and Douglas Schmidt, eds. 1995. *Pattern Languages of Program Design*. Reading, Massachusetts: Addison-Wesley.

Dart, Susan. 1992. "The Past, Present, and Future of Configuration Management." Software Engineering Institute.

———. 2000. *Configuration Management: The Missing Link in Web Engineering*. Norwood, Massachusetts: Artech House.

DeMarco, Tom, and Timothy R. Lister. 1987. *Peopleware: Productive Projects and Teams*. New York: Dorset House.

Dikel, David M., David Kane, and James R. Wilson. 2001. *Software Architecture: Organizational Principles and Patterns*. Upper Saddle River, New Jersey: Prentice Hall.

Fisher, Roger, William Ury, and Bruce Patton. 1991. *Getting to Yes: Negotiating Agreement without Giving In*. 2nd ed. New York: Penguin Books.

Fogel, Karl Franz, and Moshe Bar. 2001. *Open Source Development with CVS*. 2nd ed. Scottsdale, Arizona: Coriolis Group Books.

Fowler, Martin, Kent Beck, John Brant, William Opdyke, and Don Roberts. 1999. *Refactoring: Improving the Design of Existing Code*. The Addison-Wesley Object Technology Series. Reading, Massachusetts: Addison-Wesley.

Fowler, Martin, and Matthew Foemmel. 2002. *Continuous Integration* 2001. Available from http://www.martinfowler.com/continuousIntegration.html.

Gabriel, Richard P., and Ron Goldman. 2000. *Mob Software: The Erotic Life of Code*. Dreamsongs Press.

Gamma, Erich, Richard Helm, Ralph Johnson, and John M. Vlissides. 1995. *Design Patterns: Elements of Reusable Object-Oriented Software*. The Addison-Wesley Professional Computing Series. Reading, Massachusetts: Addison-Wesley.

Gause, Donald C., and Gerald M. Weinberg. 1990. *Are Your Lights On? How to Figure out What the Problem Really Is*. New York: Dorset House.

Goldfedder, Brandon. 2002. *The Joy of Patterns: Using Patterns for Enterprise Development*. The Software Patterns Series. Boston: Addison-Wesley.

Grinter, Rebecca. 1995. "Using a Configuration Management Tool to Coordinate Software Development." Paper read at ACM Conference on Organizational Computing Systems, August 13–16, 1995, at Milpitas, California.

Harrison, Neil, Brian Foote, and Hans Rohnert. 2000. *Pattern Languages of Program Design 4*. Software Patterns Series. Boston: Addison Wesley.

Hass, Anne Mette Jonassen. 2003. *Configuration Management Principles and Practice*. The Agile Software Development Series. Boston: Addison-Wesley.

Highsmith, Jim. 2002. *Agile Software Development Ecosystems*. The Agile Software Development Series. Boston: Addison-Wesley.

Hightower, Richard, and Nicholas Lesiecki. 2002. *Java Tools for Extreme Programming: Mastering Open Source Tools Including Ant, JUnit, and Cactus*. New York: Wiley.

Hunt, Andrew, and David Thomas. 2000. *The Pragmatic Programmer: From Journeyman to Master*. Boston: Addison-Wesley.

Hunt, Andrew, and David Thomas. 2002a. "Software Archaeology." *IEEE Software* 19 (2): 20–22.

———. 2002b. "Ubiquitous Automation." *IEEE Software* 18 (1): 11–13.

Jeffries, Ron, Ann Anderson, and Chet Hendrickson. 2001. *Extreme Programming Installed*. Boston: Addison-Wesley.

Karten, Naiomi. 1994. *Managing Expectations: Working with People Who Want More, Better, Faster, and Sooner*. New York: Dorset House.

Kernighan, Brian W., and Rob Pike. 1999. *The Practice of Programming*. The Addison-Wesley Professional Computing Series. Reading, Massachusetts: Addison-Wesley.

Krutchen, Philippe. 1995. "The 4+1 Model View of Architecture." *IEEE Software* 12 (6): 42–50.

Leon, Alexis. 2000. *A Guide to Software Configuration Management*. Norwood, Massachusetts: Artech House.

Manns, Mary Lynn, and Linda Rising. 2002. "Introducing Patterns into Organizations" 2002. Available from http://www.cs.unca.edu/~manns/intropatterns.html.

Martin, Robert C., Dirk Riehle, and Frank Buschmann. 1998. *Pattern Languages of Program Design 3*. The Software Patterns Series. Reading, Massachusetts: Addison-Wesley.

McConnell, Steve. 1993. *Code Complete: A Practical Handbook of Software Construction*. Redmond, Washington: Microsoft Press.

———. 1996. *Rapid Development: Taming Wild Software Schedules*. Redmond, Washington: Microsoft Press.

———. 2000. "What's in a Name?" *IEEE Software* 17 (5): 7–9.

———. 2002. "Closing the Gap." *IEEE Software* 19 (1): 3–5.

Mikkelsen, Tim, and Suzanne Pherigo. 1997. *Practical Software Configuration Management: The Latenight Developer's Handbook*. Upper Saddle River, New Jersey: Prentice Hall PTR.

Myers, Glenford J. 1979. *The Art of Software Testing*. New York: Wiley.

Olson, Don Sherwood, and Carol L. Stimmel. 2002. *The Manager Pool: Patterns for Radical Leadership*. Software Patterns Series. Boston: Addison-Wesley.

Oshry, Barry. 1996. *Seeing Systems: Unlocking the Mysteries of Organizational Life*. San Francisco, California: Barrett-Koehler.

Rising, Linda. 2000. *The Pattern Almanac 2000*. Software Patterns Series. Boston: Addison-Wesley.

Roche, Ted, and Larry C. Whipple. 2001. *Essential SourceSafe*. Hentzenwerke Corporation.

Schmidt, Douglas C., Michael Stal, Hans Rohnert, and Frank Buschmann. 2000. *Pattern-Oriented Software Architecture: Patterns for Concurrent and Distributed Objects*. 2nd ed. New York: Wiley.

Shaw, Mary, and David Garlan. 1996. *Software Architecture: Perspectives on an Emerging Discipline*. Upper Saddle River, New Jersey: Prentice Hall.

Tichy, Walter F. 1985. "A System for Version Control." *Software Practice and Experience* 15 (7).

Ury, William. 1993. *Getting Past No: Negotiating Your Way from Confrontation to Cooperation*. Rev. ed. New York: Bantam Books.

Vance, Stephen. 1998. "Advanced SCM Branching Strategies." Available from http://svance.solidspeed.net/steve/perforce/Branching_Strategies.html.

Vlissides, John M. 1998. *Pattern Hatching: Design Patterns Applied*. Software Patterns Series. Reading, Massachusetts: Addison-Wesley.

Vlissides, John M., James O. Coplien, and Norman L. Kerth, 1996. *Pattern Languages of Program Design 2*. Reading, Massachusetts: Addison-Wesley.

Wiegers, Karl E. 2002. "Fightin' Words." Available from http://StickyMinds. com.

Weinberg, Gerald M. 1986. *Becoming a Technical Leader.* New York: Dorset House.

————. 1991. *Quality Software Management, Volume 1: Systems Thinking.* New York: Dorset House.

————. 1993. *Quality Software Management, Volume 2: First-Order Measurement.* New York: Dorset Houe.

————. 2002. *More Secrets of Consulting: The Consultant's Tool Kit.* New York: Dorset House.

White, Brian A. 2000. *Software Configuration Management Strategies and Rational ClearCase®: A Practical Introduction.* The Addison-Wesley Object Technology Series. Boston: Addison-Wesley.

Whitgift, David. 1991. *Methods and Tools for Software Configuration Management.* Wiley Series in Software Engineering Practice. Chichester, England: Wiley.

Wingerd, Laura, and Christopher Seiwald. 1998. "High-Level Best Practices in Software Configuration Management." Paper read at Eighth International Workshop on Software Configuration Management, July 1998, at Brussels, Belgium.

# Index

# Other Patterns Resources from Addison-Wesley

0-201-63361-2

0-201-18462-1

0-201-43293-5

0-201-74397-3

0-201-65759-7

0-201-59607-5

0-201-71594-5

0-201-72583-5

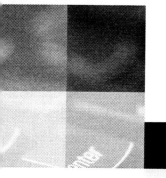

# Register
## Your Book

at www.awprofessional.com/register

**You may be eligible to receive:**

- Advance notice of forthcoming editions of the book
- Related book recommendations
- Chapter excerpts and supplements of forthcoming titles
- Information about special contests and promotions throughout the year
- Notices and reminders about author appearances, tradeshows, and online chats with special guests

## Contact us

If you are interested in writing a book or reviewing manuscripts prior to publication, please write to us at:

Editorial Department
Addison-Wesley Professional
75 Arlington Street, Suite 300
Boston, MA 02116 USA
Email: AWPro@aw.com

Visit us on the Web: http://www.awprofessional.com